Five Tickets to Kansas deeply tugged at my heart, often leaving me wanting to advocate for the innocent as I journeyed with Susan and her siblings. A tragically beautiful story of family sorrows and desperate circumstances, we see the transformation from waning hope to redeeming love. The Gospel message and the Lord's providence quietly weave through each page.

> \- Tammy McMahan, President of The Ruth Project Author of *Sword Study Series: A Family-centered Bible Study*

Five Tickets to Kansas is a fantastic narrative of anguish and redemption. It makes us see once again that there are no divine impossibilities.

> \- Valorie Quesenberry, Author of *Reflecting Beauty: Embracing the Creator's Design*

Five Tickets to Kansas is an excellent read for foster and adoptive families. As an adoptive mom, this book gave me a child's glimpses into life in traumatic situations. The feeling of being a secondary member of society, making hard decisions regarding your future, protecting your siblings, and how beautifully bio and adoptive families can work together are a few of the things that impacted me as I read. This book helps open the eyes of the caregiver to a myriad of events that affect children and their birth and adoptive families.

> \- Carla Store, Preservice Trainer for Adoptive Parents and Foster Caregivers Ohio

Five Tickets to Kansas is a true story you will never forget. Susan describes the uncertainties and horrors of being neglected while struggling to provide for and protect her siblings. The story is truly an inside look into a dysfunctional family and each members' heartache. The reader will understand healing is a gift only God can give.

> \- Marilou Kennedy, Former CASA Guardian Ad Litem (CASA: Court Appointed Special Advocate for foster children.)

After reading *Five Tickets to Kansas*, I have a more profound respect for Susan as a person and a new insight into the remarkable work Christ did for us on Calvary. I, too, long for the healing that comes from heaven. After reading this story, I am positive that His grace is sufficient and that He alone turns our darkness into marvelous light.

> \- Lynn Wilson, Friend

A remarkable journey of emotional depth, the author brings us along as she unearths her painful past and tells the bigger story of forgiveness and restoration. In a string of seemingly hopeless events, we follow a young girl through heavy darkness, coping with trials that no child should know, to a place of personal peace and reconciliation. While this book gives unwavering hope to the offended, it also offers, without apology, forgiveness and restoration to the guilty. The beauty of this page-turning book is that it is a treasure and a solid reminder of Christ's far-reaching love and redemption.

> \- Melissa Roe, Writer

Five Tickets to Kansas

A MEMOIR

SUSAN CARTER

Kaleidoscope

Massillon, Ohio, USA

Kaleidoscope Publishing

Five Tickets to Kansas by Susan Carter
Copyright © 2022 Susan Carter

ISBN: 979-8-9865367-0-5

This title is also available at www.kaleidoscopebooks.net

Requests for information should be addressed to: Kaleidoscope
Publishing, 1738 Oak Trail St. NE, Massillon, Ohio 44646

Cover photography and design: Kevin Miles Moser

For more information about the author visit
www.susancarterauthor.com

Library of Congress Cataloging-in-Publication Data
Carter, Susan
Five Tickets to Kansas/ Susan Carter 1st ed.

Printed in the United States of America

DEDICATION

To my siblings, my forever friends.

Dear Reader,

My story is one of abandonment, survival, forgiveness, and reconciliation. It is the story of heartbreak that requires a lifetime to heal.

While some individuals are oblivious to the impact their choices have on the trajectory of their lives and the lives of others, the consequences of those decisions can still ripple across multiple generations as happened in my family even before I was born. Only God knows how my life and the lives of my siblings might have been different if my parents had chosen to forgive one another. But I have learned that contemplating *what-ifs* doesn't bring healing or light to a life.

Only God can bring light, piece together our brokenness, and restore wholeness. No one is beyond His reach, as my story shows.

I admit I have changed several names, places, dates, and the order of some events—to protect some individuals who are still living and to prevent shaming others. Still, I pray my story shows the power of forgiveness. I pray my story shows healing is possible, even if it takes a lifetime.

Lovingly,
Susan

CONTENTS

PROLOGUE

May 2005, Loveland, Ohio
Susan

The call came mid-afternoon on a Friday. "Hello, Susan? This is your Aunt Sharon."

"Hello," I said.

A knot formed in the pit of my stomach. Although many years ago she had saved my younger brother from choking, Aunt Sharon had never been an integral part of my life. Still, when I'd flown to Nova Scotia to visit my father a while back, and he'd taken me to visit her, I'd given her my number.

"I'm surprised to hear from you." I tried to stay calm. Whatever news she had couldn't be good.

"I thought you should know your father passed away early this morning." Her voice remained level, controlled.

"I'm sorry to hear that."

Although his death wasn't unexpected. He'd had an internal defibrillator for three years, so I'd known his time was short. I was sad he was gone but abundantly grateful for our restored relationship. During my visit, we'd made sweet memories.

"He wanted you to sing for his funeral. It'll be next

1

Wednesday."

"I'll do my best to be there."

I hung up and began preparations for the trip. Tears of gratitude slid down my cheeks. I was thankful for the memories I shared with my father and for the hope of seeing him again in Heaven. Who would have thought I'd ever be reconciled with him? Or, with my mother?

Days later as I flew from Cincinnati to Halifax, the plane passed through a series of spring thunderstorms. The aircraft rocked and tossed its way from Chicago to Maine. Then as we crossed the Bay of Fundy, dark storm clouds clustered on the western horizon. But underneath us, a brilliant rainbow arched toward Nova Scotia. When I saw it, a sweet peace enveloped my soul, assurance that one day I would indeed see my father on the golden streets of Heaven.

CHAPTER ONE

It's Complicated

September 1961, Dartmouth, Nova Scotia
Madeline

Plagued with insomnia, at 4:30 a.m. Madeline settled into her rocker, weary in body and spirit. She patted her swollen tummy. *Will this night ever end?* Days spent chasing an active toddler and being eight months pregnant with her second child meant she was already beyond exhausted.

The phone rang. She hurried to answer, praying the noise hadn't awakened Marcus. She'd never get him back to sleep. *Please, God, not an accident.*

"Hello?"

"Good morning, love," her husband said.

Madeline breathed a sigh of relief.

"Hey. I'm at the police station," Dave said.

"You got a ticket?"

"It's a little more complicated than that. I gave one of my buddies a ride home from the bar, and he left a leather jacket in the back seat. I had no idea he stole it from another guy. When the cops stopped me for speeding, they charged me with possession of stolen goods."

"You're in jail?" Madeline's voice broke.

"Yeah. Not sure how long this will take. Might be a couple days."

"What are we gonna do? If you're not working … the rent's due next week." Dave didn't make much working as a janitor, but he did make enough. Barely.

"Calm down. I handle the bills, right?"

She caught the hint of irritation in her husband's voice and pressed her fingertips to her lips, stifling a sob.

"Maddie?"

"Okay, I'll leave you to 'er, eh?"

"Catch ya later, love."

"Yup, bye-bye," she said.

She hung up and returned to her chair. Stopped for speeding and arrested for stealing a jacket he didn't take. How bad could the penalty be?

She closed her eyes and tried to doze. When the sun rose, her son would awake, and any chance of a nap would vanish.

"I have one month to find a place to live." Madeline crumpled the eviction notice as she spoke to her mother by phone. "And I have no money for a deposit on another place."

Her worst fear had come true. Circumstantial evidence had stacked up against Dave. With no money for a defense lawyer, he'd been given the standard sentence for that type of crime—eighteen months in prison.

"Come stay with me," her mother said. "I'll ready the guest room and get out the crib."

The offer eased some of her worries, but … "You

already have renters in the attic and someone using the couch. I couldn't impose."

"You won't cramp me one bit. Besides, you'll need help with the newborn. Have you chosen a name?"

"Susan. Susan Lynn." Madeline took a deep breath. "I'll move our things to your place tomorrow."

May 1962

Madeline stepped onto the porch at her mother's home on Chebucto Road. She sat on the steps, sipping hot tea and watching the traffic. She'd never been this lonely, and the weight of it was crushing her. The last six months with Dave in prison had felt like an eternity, and his sentence was far from over.

Heels clicked on the sidewalk as her friend, Julia, rounded the corner. She'd been a sweet companion during this rough patch. Her brother had also spent time in jail, so she understood the embarrassment relatives of inmates endured.

"What's goin' on?" Julia called.

Madeline gave a tentative smile and shrugged.

Julia made her way to the white picket fence framing the yard. "You're lookin' mighty fine." She winked.

"Yeah, for an old lady." Madeline poured the remainder of her tea on the red tulips nodding in the light breeze.

"Why so glum?" Julia reached over the gate, unlatched the lock, and made her way to the porch, shooing away the cat.

Madeline scooted over and patted the space beside

her. "I'd offer you a cup of tea, but I just used the last bag."

"I'll take one next time." Julia joined her on the top step. "Do you have plans for Friday night? My sister and I are going to the pub. We shouldn't have a problem finding a sailor to buy our meal and a few drinks."

"Have fun."

"Why don't you come? Have your mum watch the babies."

"Don't be ridiculous." She rolled her eyes. "I'm married with two kids."

"You're twenty. With your dark eyes and auburn hair—"

"I shouldn't." Yet, she felt color rising in her cheeks at the thought. "Sailors in their dress whites are way too tempting for a lonely woman like me."

They sat in silence, watching kids line up outside the dilapidated Dairy Queen beside the park.

"C'mon." Julia threw her arm around Madeline's shoulders and squeezed. "One night of fun. What's the harm in that? The Split Crow serves the tastiest fish and chips in town."

Madeline hesitated. "Dave would be furious."

"Well now, he's in the clink, isn't he? You'll be with friends. It's not like you're going on a date."

Maybe it wasn't like going on a date. After all, she wasn't the one serving a sentence. So what if she wanted to enjoy life and have a few drinks?

A month later, morning sickness filled her heart with fear and regret. One careless act was now a pregnancy she wouldn't be able to hide.

November 1962
Dave

Dave held the phone firmly to his ear and counted the rings—*three, four, five*. He was also counting the days until he would get out of jail. With the holidays approaching, he missed his family more than ever. He was regularly allowed to call home, but Madeline seemed to be avoiding his calls. *Eight, nine, ten.*

"Hello?" Madeline's voice sounded frail and far away.

"Hi, love. How are you?" Relief that she'd answered rushed through him.

"Ohhh, ya know. Not bad. And yourself?"

His pulse quickened. "I'm so happy to hear your voice. Man, I miss you, Maddie. How are the kids?"

"Good. Mum made cupcakes for Susan."

"Yeah, sorry I missed her birthday. You okay?"

"Yup."

"Oh, come on, something's wrong. I hear it in your voice."

"Nope, everything's fine."

"Why haven't you been to visit me?" He struggled to keep his tone light and free of accusation. "I haven't seen you in months."

"I have two babies, plus I'm taking care of Edith's boys. That makes five kids under the age of three that I'm chasing all day long, and you ask why I'm not dropping everything and running up there to hold your hand?"

"Whoa! Calm down, love. It's just that you hardly answer when I call. I miss talking to you."

"The kids are fussing. I need to go."

"Okay, you seem pretty busy." He hoped she heard

the longing in his voice.

"Yup, gotta go."

"Take 'er easy, eh." His spirit plummeted.

"Will do."

"Love you."

"Bye-bye."

Dave slowly replaced the receiver and shuffled back to his cell. He hoped Maddie would at least visit him at Christmas, but he could feel her pulling away from him. She might never forgive him for going to prison. How could he make this up to her?

January 1963

Dave was going home a new man. He was being released early, and he was grateful for that. The long hours of solitude in a cold cell had provided him time to analyze his priorities. Thanks to his counselor, he realized spending his weekends at the bar reflected thoughtlessness and self-centeredness. Still, he fought resentment about serving time for another man's crime.

He stood outside the prison and flagged down a taxi, giving the driver his mother-in-law's address. He'd only seen pictures of his now fifteen-month-old daughter and regretted missing her first year of life.

Dave shifted on the taxi's backseat. He was sorry for being unkind and impatient with Maddie in the past. She probably considered his prison time a form of neglect. Had she been as lonely for him as he'd been for her? She must have been angry to not have visited him at Christmas. Still, he was optimistic and ready for a new beginning.

"I'll make it right," he whispered.

Their calls had become short and infrequent. He'd sensed a strain in their most recent conversations and assumed the indifference in her voice came from the long separation. But a long talk and a healthy dose of snuggle time would surely cure their communication problems.

The taxi pulled along the sidewalk. Dave paid the fare using a twenty his mother had sent him. He rapped the knocker three times and opened the door of his mother-in-law's house. The aroma of fresh-baked bread wafted in the air. Home never smelled so good.

Dave entered the kitchen. "What's goin' on, Sarah?"

His mother-in-law spun toward him and frowned.

"Didn't Maddie tell you I'd be coming home today?"

"I—I must have forgotten." Sarah brushed the hair from her cheek and smoothed her apron.

Her cool reception confused him, but he chose to hide his disappointment. "Sorry I startled you." He surveyed the kitchen. "Where's Marcus?"

"Napping," Sarah said.

He considered peeking at the four-year-old, but knew the boy needed his nap.

The plump toddler in a highchair cooed and threw a handful of Cheerios on the floor. Loose black curls framed her round face and rose-colored cheeks. She had her mother's dark eyes and his button nose.

"This must be my sweet Susan." His voice thickened with emotion.

Sarah nodded.

Dave reached for his daughter, then drew back. "Why are her hands wrapped in gauze?"

Sarah turned down the flame under the pot of boiling green beans and coughed nervously. "Susan ran down the hallway, tripped, and fell on the register."

He lifted his baby into his arms. From now on, he'd love, protect, and provide for his children every day.

Sarah pulled out a chair and sat. "She tried to break her fall and burned both palms on the heater directly above the furnace. I tell you, blisters the size of a fifty-cent piece covered both hands. The surgeon took skin grafts from her thighs." Her voice caught, and she wiped her eyes with the corner of her apron. "They said she needs to wear the bandages for two more weeks, eh?"

"*You* took her to the hospital? Where was Maddie?"

"Madeline isn't living here anymore." Sarah lowered her gaze.

Panic washed over him. "What do you mean she doesn't live here? Where's my wife?"

Sarah shook her head and looked away.

Dave tightened his hold on his baby girl. Susan wailed in fear—after all, she didn't know him. He shoved her at Sarah, then ran down the stairs and out the back door.

Hot tears coursed down his cheeks. He'd kept his sanity during the endless prison days by focusing on being reunited with Maddie. Madeline meant everything to him. Hadn't he owned his failures and resolved to be a loving and sensitive husband?

As he walked to the harbor, the blustering wind cut through his thin jeans and stung his face. An unsettling dread simmered in his soul. Why had Madeline left her mother's home? Was his wife avoiding him?

Dave used the footpath on the MacDonald Bridge to cross the bay. At the bus station, he emptied his pockets, picking through loose change and lint to gather enough coins for fare to visit his mother. Maybe she could tell him where to find his wife.

"What's goin' on?" Dave stormed into his mother's home and collapsed in the velvet recliner. "Madeline left the kids, and Sarah says she's nowhere to be found. Somebody knows where she is." His voice broke. "She's my wife for cryin' out loud."

His mother laid a hand on his shoulder. "Madeline is eight months pregnant."

Dave jerked away and stared up into his mother's face. *No!*

"Everything's hush-hush," his mum said. "Madeline moved out west and is living with her sister."

He buried his face in his hands as the room seemed to spin. If only he hadn't been so reckless with her heart. He'd sensed his wife distancing herself and worried some other man would take his place. Is that what happened? Had another man taken his place?

Dave called his sister-in-law and confirmed Madeline had sought shelter at her house. He was on his way there but didn't want her telling Maddie he was coming.

He borrowed money from his mother to purchase a train ticket to Belleville, Ontario. He climbed aboard the locomotive and took a seat by the picture window. Rain pelted against the glass, blurring the view of the beautifully forested landscape. As mile after mile rolled by, he struggled to find a balance between the pain and resentment he felt over his wife's unfaithfulness with his desire to overlook her errors. His mother had said the deep wounds of betrayal would heal with time and renewed trust.

He clenched and unclenched his jaw. His love for Madeline remained strong, and whatever the cost, he was determined not to lose her. But an illegitimate child complicated the situation. Would he be able to look at the baby each morning without seeing Madeline's infidelity? Without seeing another man's child?

Time would tell. He hoped once he and Madeline talked, the dull ache in his chest would melt away. But he had to admit the mere sight of her swollen belly might trigger jealousy. Dave shuddered as a fresh surge of melancholy and confusion settled over him like a chilling fog.

CHAPTER TWO

Happy Valentine's

January 1963, Belleville, Ontario
Madeline

Despite the cold January weather, Madeline sought solace on the front porch steps, where she often went to sip her tea. While she enjoyed being around her sister, living with a newlywed couple had become awkward. Their need for privacy left her feeling like a third wheel and intensified her loneliness. *All because of one night of indiscretion.*

She adjusted a quilt around her legs, then froze at the sound of approaching footsteps. Dave had found her. And his expression held a mixture of somberness and determination.

He's gonna kill me. He'll never truly forgive me.

She quickly poured her drink on the snow and scrambled for the house. As she opened the screen door, her husband caught up with her.

"Hey, hey." His voice was soft, his eyes glistening. He reached for her. "Everything will be alright."

Madeline trembled in his embrace, then nestled her head into his shoulder. Could this be a new beginning for them? Could she dare hope for forgiveness?

"Dave, I'm sorry."

He smoothed her hair. "Hush. Not now. Let's go somewhere warm to talk."

She suggested the Dark Bean Café. They chose a small table in the corner with the aroma of freshly ground coffee and pastries saturating the air.

"When Mum told me you were pregnant, my brain blitzed out on me," he said. "I refused to believe it."

She fidgeted with the hem of the red and white gingham tablecloth. "I made a foolish mistake."

"Why did you run away? What were you thinking?" A hint of anger crept into his tone. "You knew I was coming home."

"Again, I'm sorry. I knew you'd be angry." She sniffed back tears. "I planned to give this child up for adoption. And . . . eventually, return to Halifax." She glanced at Dave. The eyes that had earlier held kindness now clouded with indifference.

"Do you have the adoption forms?" He stretched out his upturned palm and wiggled his fingers in a give-it-here gesture.

She removed the creased and tear-stained papers from her handbag and eased them across the table.

"I'm considering raising the baby as my own," he said.

Hope flickered. She wanted to trust his words, but his expression showed no emotion. Madeline studied his face as he scanned the papers. She searched his eyes as if to see deep into his soul. He said the right things, but she couldn't tell if he meant them.

His fingers drummed on top of the forms. "No one needs to know the child isn't mine. I have confidence in my family's ability to keep the child's identity a secret."

She took her husband's hand.

"I'm not making any promises, Maddie." He pulled away, clenching and unclenching his jaw. "I'm saying I have a lot to think about." He stuffed the forms in the inner pocket of his wool jacket, then stared out the window.

Tears pooled in Madeline's eyes. For a moment, the hope of forgiveness and a fresh beginning had mocked her. Now, the shadow of resentment on Dave's face filled her with dread. Could he truly forgive her, or would she never be able to regain his trust?

February 1963
Dave

Dave sat in the waiting room of the maternity ward. "Of all days for a baby to arrive. Valentine's Day—the one day that highlights love and romance." He cursed under his breath. "Why did Madeline get us into this mess?" *I need a drink.*

Over the last few weeks, he and Maddie had struggled to reconnect. But he hadn't been able to forgive her, and she hadn't said she'd forgiven him, either. His inner turmoil and the undercurrent of distrust had kept them both on edge.

He rose and walked to the coffee machine. A poor substitute for beer, but it was all he could get right then. He loved Madeline. Maybe they could make this work. Move forward.

He returned to the waiting room, careful not to spill the lid-less coffee. This time he chose the seat farthest from the drafty window.

Dave gulped hot coffee and cursed when it burned his mouth. The child, of course, was innocent. It wasn't the baby's fault that Maddie … The child would need a decent home. If the baby was a girl, why take her from her mother and give her to a stranger? If the baby was a boy, he could carry on the family name.

A random newborn's muffled cry echoed from the opposite hallway. Jealous anger surged through his veins, drowning every thought of kindness and forgiveness. He refused to give his name to a child that wasn't his. He had a son of his own.

Dave slammed his fist into the wall, bloodying his knuckles. "What on earth was I thinking?" He swallowed the rest of his coffee, crumpled the cup, and shot it into the trash can with a flick of his wrist.

For the next two hours while his wife labored, Dave paced the hallway, contemplating his next move. Finally, he entered the birthing room, pausing by the door as the nurse handed Madeline her baby.

The nurse glanced at him. "Congratulations! You have a daughter."

Madeline's face radiated joy as she cradled her little one. "Would you like to hold her?"

Dave shook his head and walked to the far corner of the room. He leaned against the heater and glanced out the window, hoping the nurse would hurry up and leave.

"Do you have a name for this child?" the nurse asked.

Madeline traced her daughter's face with her fingertips. "Rose."

"What a beautiful name. I'm leaving this bottle of formula. Be patient as she learns to latch and suck." She handed Madeline the bottle and tucked a rolled-up blanket under her arm. "I'll be back shortly to check on you."

Madeline patiently worked to help her baby latch onto her bottle. "Mummy loves you." She pressed her lips against the baby's forehead, nuzzling and inhaling her scent.

How could Maddie have done this to him? Cheated on him? He would never forgive her.

Never.

Dave placed the adoption release forms on the portable table and wheeled it to Maddie's bed.

"What's this?" her voice quivered.

"I can't raise another man's child." He ran his hand through his hair and turned away. "Every time I see her, she'll remind me of ..." He shook with anger.

"I understand," Madeline whispered.

He placed a pen on the adoption forms and loomed over her, ensuring she signed each page.

Madeline's lower lip quivered. Finally, she pushed away the forms and focused on her daughter. "My beautiful baby girl. You are perfect in every way. I wish I could keep you and love you. I wish I could change how you were conceived."

Dave walked back to the far corner of the room and sat, planting his elbows on his knees and his chin in his hands. Hearing Maddie coo over her baby stirred a twinge of compassion in his soul, then a fresh surge of anger quickly replaced it. He wasn't to blame; Maddie had played the fool. She had done wrong. Now she would face the consequences.

"Tomorrow, your new mummy will come for you," Madeline's voice broke. Tears fell, cascading off her chin, falling to the blanket swaddling the baby. "I hope and pray she'll take good care of you. Every February fourteenth, I'll kiss your picture and say a prayer for you. Don't worry. I will never forget you, and I will always love you." She reached out to Dave. "The camera's in my purse. Please snap a picture of me with Rose. At least I'll have that to remember her by, right?"

"Are you joking?" He sprang from his chair and headed for the door. "I can't wait to get out of here and leave all this behind. We don't need any visual reminders of this nightmare."

Madeline

Madeline stared at the blank ceiling of her hospital room. Rose's adoptive mother would soon come to carry her home. Would her new parents ever tell Rose she had another mother?

A lead weight of gloom pressed down on Madeline. She yearned to stay in touch with her child but knew Dave wouldn't allow it. She closed her eyes. *I pray you will be healthy and strong. I pray they will love you as their own. I pray you will come back to me one day.*

After Rose was taken away, Dave arrived, and Madeline prepared to leave the hospital. As the main hospital door slid open, frigid air blasted her. She shuffled forward, pressing her hands to her empty belly. *My baby, my darling baby. What will become of you?* A river of tears froze on her face.

"Dry it up," Dave said.

Madeline groaned. The pain and grief intensified— how would she bear it?

"We will never talk of this again." His expression hardened. "Don't you dare say her name, even in a whisper." He squeezed her arm until she cried out in pain. "If my children ever learn of this child, I'll throw you out on the street. Do you understand?"

"Yep." Madeline inhaled deeply. *Rose, forgive me.*

Madeline stumbled and fell onto a wooden bench outside the hospital entryway. All her strength seemed to have drained away.

"Wait 'til I have you back home," Dave continued. "I promise to make your life miserable."

Madeline buried her face in her hands and sobbed.

Susan Carter

CHAPTER THREE

Lazy Days of Summer

July 1964, Dartmouth, Nova Scotia
Susan

Like we did so often, Mum and Dad piled all of us into our green Ford station wagon, and we headed for the ocean. I sat in the back with Marcus, the picnic basket between us. We took turns lifting the lid and snitching blueberries.

We chose our favorite spot, a dip in the dunes surrounded by seagrass. Then Dad left for work, taking the car.

Mum unpacked our gear, spread out towels, and organized our belongings. Baby Polly, only three months old, cooed in the shade of the beach umbrella. I ran along the surf with my brother, chasing sandpipers and collecting seashells. As the morning wore on and the sun warmed the sand, we moved into the water and raced the foaming waves to the shore.

When Mum called us for lunch, I loaded my hot dog with mustard, giggling as sweet relish oozed out the side of the bun and ran down my chin. A gust of wind sprinkled the baked beans with fine sand, making them gritty, but I didn't care. The constant breeze brushed against my skin and swept my hair from my face. A symphony of cawing seagulls, crashing waves, and laughter from nearby campsites made the day seem perfect.

After lunch, Marcus and I joined Mum and Polly for a splash war in a shallow pool along the surf. Then Mum settled Polly for her nap and helped me and my brother build a sandcastle.

"The secret to constructing a sturdy castle," she said, "is to use drippy sand." She dug a hole close to the surf where every wave delivered a fresh supply of water.

Mum drew a circle on the ground. "Take turns dumping your buckets on this spot." When she was satisfied with the height of our sandcastle, she used a toy shovel to carve steps up the side and a parapet edge on the tower.

I knelt beside Mum, admiring her handiwork. "Is it done?"

"Not quite," she said. She scooped arches in the walls along the stairway using a plastic spoon.

I clapped my hands. "A princess tower."

"It's a fortress," Marcus said. He smoothed an entrance to the castle. "Let's use the driftwood to line the path."

Mum placed a variety of shells around the base and on top of the towers.

Sand flew in every direction as I ran in gleeful circles around my family and our creation. "It's the best castle in the whole world!"

"The best, the best, the best!" Marcus and I chanted.

"I can't wait 'til Dad comes, so he can see it," Marcus said.

Mum shielded her eyes with her hand. "The tide's rising. Perhaps we should take a picture."

"Take one now, Mum," Marcus said.

Mum searched through our bags. "Oh, dear. I left the camera in the car. Sorry, kids." She settled down on the blanket and stroked her tummy. "We'll have another baby next winter."

"A Christmas baby." Marcus clapped his hands.

"No, a Valentine's baby." Mum stared out to sea with a far-away look in her eyes and brushed aside a tear.

I glanced at Polly. "Why do we need *another* baby?"

"Sometimes babies come close together," Mum said. "When two babies are born within the same year, they're called Irish twins."

I giggled. "We're not Irish."

The surf crept closer and closer. Mum folded the umbrella and moved our things higher on the dune.

"The ocean is touching our castle!" I cried, scrubbing my eyes with my fists. But my tears did not stop the waves from lapping away at our creation. The last indefinable lump of sand melted into the surf a short time later.

Mum massaged her temples. "Tomorrow, you can draw a picture of our castle."

The sun sank below the horizon, fading the pinkish clouds to a dull gray.

Marcus muttered. "We're the last family here."

Mum stood. "Your father will come soon."

I shivered as the temperature dropped and cinched my sweater. "My tummy's growling."

The familiar putt-putt of our Ford caught my attention. Dad drove through the surf, sending a spray of water from both sides of the car.

I leaped to my feet and waved with excitement. My dad, right on time.

The next day, I sat at the kitchen table quietly eating my breakfast. I stripped the peel from a banana and popped the fruit in my mouth.

Dad sat across from me and tapped his foot. "Hurry up with those eggs, eh, Maddie?"

Mum added a splash of milk to scrambled eggs and poured the mixture into a frying pan. She gently tossed them until they were fluffy and placed the meal before my father.

Dad harrumphed. "Where's the ketchup?"

Mum set a bottle of ketchup within Dad's reach. "Beautiful weather today. Maybe we can take the kids down to the bay and ride the ferry? They enjoy being on the water."

"Can't. I promised mother I'd come by today." Dad poured ketchup on his eggs.

Mum stared at the floor, lowered her voice, and spoke with a measured beat. "You visit her every weekend."

Dad took a swig of coffee.

Mum crossed her arms. "Once you finish at your mother's, you're going to the bar, aren't you?"

"Maddie, get off my back. Mother's car needs an oil change."

Mum pinched her lips.

Several hours later, Mum put Polly in the baby carriage. "Come, children, I need you to hold tightly on either side of the stroller."

We trudged down the hill, past the grocery store and five lights. The relentless sun beat on my head, heating my dark hair. My calves ached and blisters formed on my heels.

"A few more steps. We're almost there," Mum kept repeating.

I felt we walked a hundred miles.

Finally, we stopped outside a bar. Marcus and I stood by the carriage while Mum went inside to speak to Dad.

A few moments later, Mum returned and sat on the curb. "Your father's playing pool. He'll be along soon."

I rubbed my face. "The smoke from the cars stings my nose."

"Mine, too," Marcus said.

Mum patted the curbside, indicating we should sit with her. "Why don't you play the hold-your-breath-as-long-as-you-can game?"

Just when I thought we could wait no longer, Dad appeared and escorted us to the restaurant across the street. When we stepped inside, Marcus and I grinned.

"Wow," I said. "Look at the fancy checkered tablecloths and shiny forks."

My brother and I held hands and followed our hostess to our seats. Within minutes, the waitress served us plates of piping hot home fries smothered in beef gravy.

Mum's forehead wrinkled with worry. "The electric bill is due next Tuesday."

Dad ordered a slice of raisin pie with a flaky, golden crust for my brother and me to share. My mouth watered in anticipation.

Mum tapped the side of her teacup. "No power means no watching ball games on TV."

Dad gave one last puff on his cigarette and dropped the butt in Mum's drink. "I'm umping tonight. The game starts in half an hour. I won't have time to drive you home."

Mum balled her napkin in her fist. She looked unhappy and worried.

Why were my parents always fighting?

I chewed the last bite of raisin pie and beamed at Dad.

He winked back at me.

But I had worries of my own. The rest of us still had to walk home. As I shuffled beside Marcus and followed Mum, the streetlights blinked on. The blisters on my heels broke and wet my socks. Hot tears rolled down my cheeks.

"I hate walking," Marcus said.

I fell to my knees. "Carry me, Mummy. Pleeease!"

Mum stopped the baby carriage and jerked me to my feet. "You're almost three years old. Walk." She turned her head, brushing away her tears.

When we arrived home, Mum put band-aids on my heels and readied us for bed. "If you go right to sleep, we'll go to the Dominion Day Festivities tomorrow."

"Yay, fireworks!" I said.

"I hope we sit on Citadel Hill," Marcus said. "We'll have the best view of the whole bay and won't miss a thing."

"Settle down, please." Mum left us, closing the bedroom door.

I pulled the sheet up to my neck. "I'm taking my blankie," I whispered.

Madeline

With her children tucked into bed, Madeline finally had a moment to herself. She walked to the television and turned up the volume.

"I loved you from the first moment I met you," a male actor said.

"My darling, I love you, too," the actress responded.

Madeline pressed her hand to her lips, holding back a sob as loneliness washed over her. She clicked off the TV, went to her desk, and searched for pen and paper. Tears splashed on the page as she wrote a letter to her closest friend.

Dearest Mum,

I fed Polly a bottle of warm milk and put the kids to bed. I have my hands full twenty-four hours a day. Dave is out umpiring another ball game. I guarantee he will return to the bar before coming home. The children won't listen to me. Not five minutes ago, I gave Marcus and Susan a talking to, and they're still joking and whispering instead of going to sleep. I feel like a single parent, right? I'm losing it to the point of breaking.

P.S. I'm pregnant. It's twins. If they are girls, I'll call them Coleen and Claire.

All my love,
Maddie

Five Tickets to Kansas

CHAPTER FOUR

Baby Blues

April 1965, Hamilton, Ontario
Madeline

As she once again handled all the evening tasks at home alone, Madeline knew she'd reached her limit. Although Dave had moved their family to take a high-paying job, he still didn't come home to her at night after work. No, he treated himself to after-work drinks at the bar.

Her newborn twins, only six weeks old, were colicky and cried all the time. So, she cried all the time, too. Even eating took too much energy. She simply couldn't take one more day of all this responsibility and pressure. Once while grocery shopping, she'd had a meltdown while trying to choose a brand of pasta.

That had gotten Dave's attention. He'd taken her to the medical clinic. The doctor diagnosed her with postpartum depression.

Madeline tucked Susan in bed with Marcus. As usual, when she leaned in and kissed their foreheads, Susan sniffed, breathing in the sweetness of her lily-scented perfume. Madeline turned and walked to the closet to retrieve the battered suitcase from the top shelf. There was only so much a woman could take.

"What's Mum doing?" she heard Susan whisper to her brother.

"I'll be sitting on the front porch," Madeline whispered. "I'm warning you kids, be quiet. Your father will be home soon, and he'd better find you sleeping." She finger-waved goodbye and turned off the light.

Dave

As he did every night when he arrived home from the bar, Dave paused briefly at each bedroom to check on his sleeping children. Upon entering the darkened master bedroom, he lowered himself to the mattress and reached for his wife.

"What in the world?" he threw back the covers and flipped on the light.

Empty. The bed was empty. But a slip of pink stationery leaned against the lamp on the nightstand. The message read *I need time alone.*

Dave crumpled the note and threw it at his wedding photo. He swung around and knocked over the bedside lamp, sending it crashing to the floor. For the rest of the night, he paced in the living room, dropping cigarette ashes on the carpet.

Susan

The following day, I shared the umbrella with Marcus as we waited to load into the taxi. "Where's Mum? Isn't she coming with us?"

Baby Claire let out a wail, and Dad worked feverishly to console her.

"Where are we going?" I whispered to Marcus.

"To Grandma's house in Dartmouth."

"How do you know?"

"I heard Dad talking on the phone."

"I don't remember Grandma."

"Of course not. You were only a baby when we lived there."

"How old were you?"

"I'm two years older than you." Marcus used his I'm-the-big-brother voice.

We piled into the train station, and Dad bought tickets to Halifax, Nova Scotia. I bounced on my toes. "We're riding on a train."

Our house in Hamilton sat next to a railroad. Often while playing, my brother and I would stop to watch the trains flying down the track. The way the ground shook told me the train engine was drawing near. We would wave as the train passed, calling, "Hello, everyone! Hello!"

Sometimes the passengers waved back. Now, on this trip to Grandma's, we were the passengers.

The swaying train jostled us from side to side. When allowed, we took turns walking up and down the aisle like drunken sailors. A man in a brown velvet rabbit suit passed through our cabin about mid-day. He wore a light blue jacket and held a wicker basket full of chocolate Easter eggs.

Marcus whispered in my ear. "That's Peter Rabbit."

I grinned at him. "'Magine, Peter Rabbit, on our train!"

Peter Rabbit stopped at our seat, and I smelled the chocolate he carried. "Would you youngsters like some candy?" He dipped his hand into the wicker basket and offered us chocolate eggs filled with marshmallow cream.

I reached for candy, and so did Marcus. "Thank you," we said.

My younger sister, Polly, kept her face buried behind Dad's arm.

Peter Rabbit tried to coax her from her hiding place. "Now, little one," he said, "I have a special treat for you." He offered a yellow marshmallow peep and lowered his voice. "Will you take the candy, Princess?"

Polly peeked out just as Peter Rabbit leaned over the seat. His floppy ears swung forward and hit her in the face. She wailed and hid again in Dad's armpit.

Dad shifted his hold on Coleen and reached for the candy. "I'll save it for her." He stuffed the treat in his coat pocket.

I settled into my seat and unwrapped the Easter egg. I nibbled the chocolate until I found the center, then poked my tongue into the creamy marshmallow, smiling with contentment. Peter Rabbit, chocolate, and trains. What could be better? If only Dad wasn't so upset, and I knew where Mum had gone.

Dave

Dave sat on the train, watching over his children. The constant motion finally rocked all five kids to sleep. He surveyed the other passengers in the cabin.

A young couple sat three rows in front of him. Dave watched as the gentleman doted on his wife. He retrieved a blanket from the overhead luggage and covered his wife's legs. Later he brought her a hot chocolate from the food bar, and the couple swapped seats to give the woman extra legroom.

Dave's thoughts went to Madeline. True, he hadn't pampered her. But, no one had coddled *his* mother, and she got along just fine.

He smirked. Maddie's responsibility was caring for the kids, and he put food on the table. Sure, he barhopped every night, but only after the kids were in bed. Her depression didn't excuse her bailing on the family.

Dave handed his ticket to the conductor. He'd lose his job over this—an unscheduled leave of absence. But what else could he do?

Claire whimpered and sucked her fist. Dave reached for the diaper bag between his feet, withdrew a bottle of formula, and pressed it to her mouth. He couldn't care for all the kids on his own and work, so taking them to his mother's was his only option.

Coleen woke. He retrieved a second bottle and offered it to Coleen. As the train wove through the countryside, he gazed out the window, formulating a plan for reconciliation with his wife.

A few hours later, the train pulled into the station. The blast of the whistle woke the children. Dave draped the diaper bag over his shoulder and carried a twin in each arm.

"Marcus and Susan, take hold of Polly's hands."

Snowflakes fell softly on his young family as they disembarked the train at the Halifax station and flagged another taxi.

Dartmouth, Nova Scotia
Susan

Dad didn't bother to knock on Grandma's front door. He simply opened it and ushered us into the living room. Grandma was talking on the phone.

"This is Goldie speaking," Grandma said. She covered the receiver. "What's goin' on?" She whispered to Dad. "Where's Madeline?"

Dad sank into the velvet recliner and positioned a twin in each arm.

Grandma hung up and locked eyes with Dad. "Where ... is ... Madeline?"

"Is that apple pie I smell?" he asked.

"Answer my question," Grandma said.

"Please help me with these screaming babies."

Grandma scooped Claire into her arms.

"She left me, Mum." Dad hung his head and covered his face with his hands.

I didn't like the dark wallpaper and dark furniture in Grandma Goldie's home, but the house was warm and smelled nice. Mum would come back ... of course, she would. I just didn't know when.

Grandma clicked her tongue. "I can't understand how a mother can just up and leave her children." She gently rocked Claire. "'Magine! And these babies are only six weeks old. What on earth was she thinkin'?"

Discouragement etched Dad's face. "The doctor said she had a case of baby blues."

"Oh, me nerves. Baby blues is a sickness of the mind.

It's simply an excuse to be irresponsible."

"Don't blame Maddie. Her constant migraines made her nauseous. She couldn't eat. The smallest decision, like which type of soup to buy or what clothes to wear, brought her to tears." Dad motioned to the twins. "Add to that, millions of dirty diapers and colic. Mum, I've got to find her."

"Phew." Grandma wrinkled her nose and pointed to the diaper bag. "Pass that here." She changed Claire's diaper. "Who's been watching the kids?"

"Madeline's sister helps out occasionally." Dad squirmed. "Well, to be honest, the kids take care of themselves. Marcus is in kindergarten." Dad gave Marcus one of his Daddy's-proud-of-you smiles. Marcus ran over to sit on Dad's knee.

"You've got to help me, Mum, at least until I find Maddie and bring her home."

"I'll think about it while I'm fixin' dinner. I'll let you know my decision after everyone's fed. But first, we need to clean up these kids."

I tiptoed across the room and leaned against Dad's chair. I didn't know what Grandma had in mind.

"Get over here, Marcus," Grandma said. "And take off your clothes."

"What am I gonna wear?" Marcus grimaced. "We didn't bring anything extra."

Grandma knelt in front of Marcus and unbuttoned his shirt. "You can dance around in your underwear for the time being." Grandma threw his clothes into a pile.

As she came toward me, I stepped back and crossed my arms. "No. I don't want to dance in my underwear."

"You'll do as you're told, young lady."

I shot out my bottom lip and stomped my foot on the

hardwood floor. *Wham!* Grandma's hand smacked my bottom. *Whoa!* I blinked back tears.

Grandma removed my undershirt. "If you're chilly, go stand on the register in the living room."

She made us dinner. Everyone finished and left the table but me. I moved my fork in circles on my plate, pushing around a lump of buttered turnips, while Grandma washed the last of the pots and pans and wiped off the counters and stovetop. Next, she retrieved the laundry basket filled with our wet clothes and draped them over a string hanging mere inches above the flames of the gas stove.

The phone in the hall rang; Grandma answered it. "Hello, Goldie speaking." She pointed at me. "Young lady," she whispered, "don't you dare move until every last bite is gone."

Mum wouldn't make me eat these yucky turnips. I glared at the laundry. *I hope those clothes fall off and burn.*

To my astonishment, an undershirt slid off the line and onto the fire. Smoke seeped its way around the shirt and rose. The T-shirt turned a light brown, then black, then burst into flame. I held my breath. In a matter of seconds, smoke rolled across the ceiling toward the door and billowed into the hallway.

Grandma rushed into the kitchen, directing her piercing glare at me. "You, naughty girl. Why didn't you call me?" She turned off the stove and opened the window.

I buried my face in the crook of my arm and sobbed. I didn't want to be there. When would Mum come to take us home?

When Grandma left the kitchen again, I tucked the last piece of bitter turnip under my tongue, tiptoed into the washroom, and spat the nasty vegetable into the trash can.

Then I went to the living room and slipped behind Dad's chair in time to hear the end of their conversation.

"You'll care for them, Mum?" Dad asked.

"Well, I can't take all five." Grandma's tone was firm. "A newborn is a full-time job. I'll ask Letty if she'll take the twins."

Grandma had converted her home into a duplex and gained a residual income. The deal sweetened when her daughter, Letty, became her upstairs tenant.

Aunt Letty had joined them in the living room and now held Coleen to her bosom. Of course, she wanted the babies. She had two self-sufficient teenagers and an independent five-year-old, so she had the extra time needed to care for the newborns.

I followed my aunt upstairs and stood near as she changed the baby's diaper. Hundreds of tiny blisters and welts covered her red and swollen bottom. "Aww, there now," Aunt Letty said. "No wonder you're crying."

Bang! The front door slammed. Panic surged through me. Had Dad left us?

I dashed back downstairs. Grandma clanged pots in the kitchen, while Marcus and Polly played with blocks in the bedroom. Everyone but me seemed oblivious to the crisis.

Dad, did you leave us, too? Where did you go?

I ran to the doily-covered sofa by the window and pulled my chubby, three-and-a-half-year-old self, up and onto its cushions. Reaching over the back of the couch, I drew aside the lace curtain. Streaks of rain on the windowpane made seeing difficult. Tears blurred my vision, further hindering my search for dad's dark coat, which blended with the gray landscape. Straining to see, I pressed my face against the window.

My stomach tightened into knots. Dad's long strides took him farther and farther away. I could never catch him. He walked too fast.

Wait for me. Don't leave me here. I held my hand over my mouth, muffling my cries. I didn't want to set off another blip on Grandma's radar.

Then, Dad disappeared over the hill.

"Get your grimy feet off my chesterfield," Grandma bellowed behind me.

I wiped my nose on my sleeve and slid down the couch to sit. For an eternity, I stayed there staring at my hands.

How long would Dad be gone? Where was Mum? And would I survive living with my grumpy Grandma?

June 1965, Great Breton Island
Dave

At a cabin in Cape Breton, Dave sat with his wife on the veranda listening to the rhythm of the crashing waves and enjoying the pine-scented air.

"I got a janitorial job." He'd looked and looked until he found his wife. He wanted to keep his family together, and he really did love Madeline.

"Where will we live?" Madeline asked.

"I've leased an apartment on Victoria Street. A ten-minute walk from work."

"I don't want to live on the Dartmouth side."

"The ferry is close. Only half an hour to your mother's."

Madeline stirred cream and sugar into her hot tea.

"Maddie, I'm not like my father."

"Hmmm."

Dave waited for a lull in the chorus of seals barking on the rocks below. "Every relationship has rough times."

Madeline rolled her eyes.

"Okay … Think of the kids. I can't raise them on my own."

July 1965, Dartmouth, Nova Scotia
Susan

A yellow taxi pulled up to the curb outside Grandma's house.

"Mummy, Mummy, Mummy!" I cried. Marcus and I ran down the steps to meet her.

Mum caught me in her arms and kissed my cheek. "Have you been a good girl?"

"Uh-huh." I smiled shyly.

Grandma stacked our belongings by the door. "You're all set." She stood in the doorway, blocking us from going back inside.

"What's the rush?" Dad asked.

"I've got things to do." Grandma reached for the doorknob.

Mum craned her neck, looking past Grandma to the foyer, which led to the upstairs apartment. "Where are the twins?"

"You abandoned the twins," Aunt Letty called from inside the house. "You'll have to take me to court to get them back."

Mum gasped. "You can't keep my babies."

"Get your foot off my doorstep," Grandma said.

I cringed at Grandma's I'm-gonna-whoop-you tone. She was mad at Mum and didn't try to hide it.

Dad grabbed Mum's arm and drew her back. "Wait, Maddie. This could be a good idea. Give yourself time to regain your strength. When you're ready, we'll return with the police."

Dad wrapped his arm around her waist and gently led her back to the taxi. Mum looked so disheartened.

I was thrilled to get into the taxi with Mum and ride away from Grandma's. I didn't understand why the twins didn't come with us, and I was confused by the adults fighting over them as children did over toys.

But Mum was back, and everything would be alright, wouldn't it?

We arrived at our apartment, bigger than we'd ever had. A large stairway led up to our new home in a building that held six apartments. Excitement bubbled in me at the thought of making lots of new friends. We'd be happy here, wouldn't we?

CHAPTER FIVE

Giggles and Tears

Spring 1967, Halifax, Nova Scotia
Susan

My twin sisters didn't come to live with us but stayed with
Aunt Letty. Mum gave birth to Davie and, a year later, to
Thomas. And so, our family continued to grow.

Dad seemed to enjoy his job as a janitor at the high
school. Mum spent her days watching the boys or sharing
tea and conversation with her friends. Marcus graduated to
third grade, and I started kindergarten.

The highlight of my life was the frequent bus trips we
took across the river to visit my mother's mother, Grandma
Nan, on the Halifax side of the harbor. I alternated weekend
sleepovers at Nan's with Marcus.

On this particular weekend, I watched Grandma Nan
add cream and two lumps of sugar to her cup of tea. Nanny
Giggles, we called her. She giggled while watching us
devour her delicious cooking. She laughed when we jumped
on the bed. And when the neighbor's cat chased her
obnoxious Mexican Chihuahua around the yard, Nan
chuckled so hard tears spilled down her cheeks and dripped

off her chin. Nan weighed only ninety-five pounds, but her five-foot-two-inch frame exuded happiness.

Nan and I cozied together in an oversized rocking chair. "Just like two peas in a pod, eh?" She giggled, then set her steaming drink on the end table and turned the TV channel to her favorite show. When the final notes of the *Mission Impossible* theme song faded, Nan tenderly kissed my forehead. "Time for bed, Do-Bee."

I stepped from the footstool to the sideboard and, gripping the sheets, pulled myself onto the mattress. My body sank into a soft cloud of extra padding and feather pillows.

Nan tucked the down-filled quilt under my chin and along my side. Kneeling by the bed, she recited the Lord's Prayer. She turned off the bedside lamp, kissed me softly on the cheek, and left the room. She cracked the door just enough for the hall light to make a thin line across the foot of the bed, our signal that she would return shortly. A fact I seldom stayed awake to verify.

The next day, Nan and I walked downtown and paid her bills at the Utility office. Between stops at the Power and Hydro Companies, we shopped at the grocery store, the bakery, and the Five and Dime. Each purchase went into the little shopping cart Nan pulled behind her.

"Would you like to feed the ducks?" Nan asked.

I jumped for joy.

We made our way along the six-foot, wrought iron fence encircling the Public Gardens to an ornate gate located on the corner of the block. Inside the park, we meandered through a maze of paved walkways, past fragrant flower beds, colorful gazebos, and a babbling stream. Nan chose a shaded bench beside the pond and pulled a bag of breadcrumbs from her handbag. While I scattered crumbs on the water, Nan giggled at the mallard ducks who quacked and fussed like squabbling siblings, racing to the food.

I held back a handful of crumbs for my favorite, the graceful white swans. They effortlessly glided across the water, holding their regal necks high as if in total command of the lake. They seemed undisturbed by the commotion of their noisy neighbors.

A flock of pigeons flew over our heads and landed at my feet.

"They want peanuts," I said.

Nan dug in her purse and handed me a dime to buy a handful of nuts from the dispenser.

I threw the peanuts toward the sky and watched the pigeons eat them mid-air.

Blissful, I returned to the bench and snuggled next to Nan. Bluebirds sang in the branches, and pansies wobbled in the breeze. A myriad of people wandered past; it seemed to me they were all smiling.

Nan patted my knee with her usual love and affection, both of which I craved. I wished I could stay there forever at my favorite park with my favorite person.

Spring 1968, Dartmouth, Nova Scotia

Two things became a regular part of my life. If my parents were home, they fought about money. And, they were rarely home.

On the nights Dad hung out at the bars, Mum told Marcus and me to watch over our younger siblings while she went to her friend's house for tea.

"You're both in school now," Mum often said. "You can handle more responsibility."

One day, I sprawled on the couch beside Marcus as *The Flying Nun* blared from the TV. Thomas napped while Polly and Davie played in the dining room. I checked on them during a commercial break and, to my dismay, found crayons strewn all over the floor and large circular scribbles covering an entire wall.

I placed my hands firmly on my hips. "Dad will whoop you good for this."

Polly and Davie dropped their crayons and retreated to the bedroom.

First, I tried wiping the crayon with a rag. But that didn't work. Then I remembered Nan's favorite go-to cleanser, Comet. I filled a bucket with warm water and dumped in the entire container of Comet. A cloud of powdery dust filled the air and coated the inside of my nostrils.

I scrubbed, and the crayon marks faded, which was good. Unfortunately, I was standing in a small lake of Comet water. Nan's solution for wet floors? Cover them with newspapers to absorb the water. I beamed with pride. Nan had taught me so many things about housekeeping.

Dad arrived a couple of hours later and stared at the decoupaged floor. "What's this?" He lifted the paper to find the Comet had dissolved the varnish and eaten through to the beautiful oak floor. The floorboards were now bleached.

"We just lost our deposit," he said through gritted teeth. His dark eyes searched our faces. "Who did this?"

Marcus sat perfectly still.

I raised a trembling hand.

My parents often left Marcus and me in charge of our siblings in the evenings. For the past several weeks, our family dentist often sat in the parking lot, waiting until Dad left for the bar and Mum went to her friend's house, then he ascended the stairs to our apartment. Whichever child happened to be on night watch received his unwanted attention.

One night after Mum and Dad left, I peered through the window, examining the cars in the parking lot. I didn't see the dentist's car, so I thought we were safe for the moment. I opened a sleeve of saltines and returned to the living room. Marcus sat on the sofa, chewing his nails.

"His car's not here," I said.

Marcus patted the space beside him. "He's coming."

"We should tell Mum and Dad."

"No."

I licked the salt off my cracker. "Let's lock the door."

He smirked. "Right. Because then Mum and Dad can't get in."

I studied his face as he gnawed his nail to the quick. The light had gone out of his eyes, and tightness had formed around his mouth. He smacked as he sucked on his bleeding finger.

I held up the saltines. "Want a cracker?"

My brother shook his head.

I sighed. "I'm going to bed."

Marcus turned his attention to the fingers on the other hand.

In my bedroom, I left the door cracked to listen for footsteps on the stairs. I searched in vain for a nightgown, gave up looking, and went to bed in my underwear.

On a Sunday afternoon, I chased Marcus around the table for the umpteenth time.

"Help me dress the boys," Mum called to the two of us. "Nan has invited us over for dinner."

"Yippee!" I cried along with Marcus.

He squeezed my arm. "What a day, Susan! What a day!"

I tackled Thomas, stripped off his dirty shirt, and replaced it with a clean one.

The journey from our apartment in Dartmouth to Nan's house in Halifax included a ferry ride. After a ten-minute walk to the docks, we stood along the waterfront and listened to the blasting fog horns and the cawing of seagulls. As we entered the ferry, the smell of wood and salty seawater greeted us. We made our way to the oak benches along either side of the cabin, the wooden planks slightly creaking underfoot. My brother beside me, I strained to see through the scratched, large glass windows and murky seawater. I couldn't see out, neither of us could, but we didn't care. We were thrilled to be on the ferry.

I waited for the throb of the engine, signaling our departure. Moments later, the boat vibrated and glided away from the dock. Muffled slapping of the waves against the hull accompanied the rise and fall of the swells. I leaned against the hard bench, smiling with contentment.

When we reached the opposite shore, the excitement of seeing Nan made the walk up the hill to Chebucto Street seem effortless. As we entered Nan's yard, we caught the aroma of freshly baked bread through the open window.

Nan busied herself about the kitchen cooking dinner. She winked at me. "Do-Bee, please help me mash these yams."

I stood on the wooden step stool and gripped the cold

masher. Although I gagged at the thought of bitter yams, I was bursting with pride. *I am Nan's helper.*

My grandmother cut the bread into thick slices then placed them beside the homemade huckleberry jam. I remembered picking those berries. We had driven a long way out into the country to Nan's cousin's house. Nan brought along plastic ice cream buckets to hold the berries. We had knelt on the rocky terrain and picked the berries from the bushes.

Now, she slammed the oven door, and she set the gingerbread on the cooling rack. The aroma filled the room. One day, she would give me the secret family recipe. We ate a dinner of mashed yams, lima beans, and sausage. For dessert, Nan served the warm gingerbread slathered with melted butter, along with glasses of cold milk.

Later, we lingered at Nan's door, saying our goodbyes. I hugged her waist and buried my face in her apron. "Please let me stay with you."

Marcus ran over and joined our hug. "Let me stay, too."

Nan stroked my hair. "Sorry. You both have school tomorrow."

"But Nan, I have a secret to tell you," I said.

Marcus pinched my arm.

"Now, now. Don't cry, Do-Bee," Nan said. "If you're here, who'll help your mum with the little ones?"

"Besides, it's *my* turn to stay with Nan," Marcus said.

Davie took my hand, and we turned toward the street. Marcus hugged Nan goodbye and followed me.

One night a month later, Marcus shook me awake. I bolted upright.

"What's goin' on?" I asked.

My brother rested his elbows on the bed and leaned in. "The police are here. Mum and Dad came home and caught the dentist in the living room with Polly. Dad called the police." Marcus reached for my hand. "Now, the cops will want to talk with you."

Sweat tingled on my palms, and somersaults tightened in my tummy. The secret we'd kept from Nan was finally out. "I don't wanna talk to them," I said, my voice quivering.

"You don't have to say anything. Just nod."

Mum entered the bedroom, her face drawn and tear-stained. "Were you—did he?"

I nodded.

Mum collapsed onto the bed and covered her face. I breathed in her Lily of the Valley perfume and waited. After Mum gained her composure, I followed her to the living room.

The policeman frowned. "We have three separate counts of child molestation."

Dad's jaw clenched and unclenched.

"No doubt this guy will be in for several years." The officer tapped his pen on his notepad.

My cheeks burned with shame. Discussing the unthinkable with an adult was embarrassing enough. But even more humiliating, I was standing in front of a policeman in the underpants I'd been sleeping in! I took a seat on the couch and folded my arms, securing my hands in my armpits and covering as much of myself as possible.

CHAPTER SIX

Major Move

Summer 1968, Dartmouth, Nova Scotia
Susan

I sat on the front steps of Grandma Goldie's porch, watching
Dad work on her Ford. He had spread out his tools on the
driveway and popped the hood of her car. Now, he grabbed
a wrench and leaned over the engine. We would be there for
a while.

I wished I were at Nan's house instead. With any
luck, Grandma would never know I was there. I slipped
around to the backyard, where I found the twins sitting on
the porch steps mixing dirt and water.

"Mud pies?" I asked cheerfully.

They nodded.

"We need dandelions to decorate the top." I grabbed
a fistful of weeds.

Coleen stood and reached for a wicker basket. We
crisscrossed the yard, gathering flowers.

"You take off the blossoms like this." I held the stem
and flipped off the top with my thumb. "Pop."

Coleen laughed. We filled her basket then returned to

the steps to decorate the pies.

"Place the dandelion tops on the pies sunny side up and gently pat them down," I said.

Claire handed me the flower tops, and I arranged them on the mud patties.

"You guys finish the dessert. I'll make dandelion stew," I said.

"How do you do that?" Claire asked.

"First, fill a pan with water, then tear the stems apart. Let them sit in the water until they curl like macaroni."

A few moments later, Claire squealed with delight. "Dandelion stew."

"Sometimes, I add pebbles for taste," I said.

The twins laughed. We joined hands and danced in a circle.

"We like playing with you, Susan!" Coleen exclaimed. "I wish we were sisters."

"We are."

The twins froze. "No, we're not," they said in unison.

"We have the same Mum and Dad. That makes us sisters."

"You're fibbing. I'm telling on you." Claire spun on her heels, hurried up the stairs, and ran into the house.

Coleen crumpled on the steps and cried.

Grandma and Aunt Letty burst through the back door and stood on the porch, towering over me. Aunt Letty wrung her hands in her apron and glared at me.

"Susan, what did you tell these children?" Grandma's icy tone sent a shiver down my spine.

"I only said . . ." *the truth.*

Grandma shook her finger at me. "Can't you see how you've upset your cousins?"

Claire wrapped her arms around Grandma's legs and

whimpered while Coleen ran into Aunt Letty's open arms. Grandma and Aunt Letty exchanged glances.

Was I really in trouble for telling the truth?

"Don't you ever speak of this again. Do you understand?" Grandma said.

"Yes," I said.

Aunt Letty bent and kissed Coleen and Claire on the cheek. "There now, Sweet Peas. Everything's alright. Go back to your game."

The adults retreated inside, and the twins resumed their play.

Why all the secrecy? My desire to play vanished. I made my way to the front yard and sat by our car, waiting for Dad to finish working on Grandma's car, so we could go home.

Fall 1968, Dartmouth, Nova Scotia

On Sunday afternoons, my family typically enjoyed leisurely drives in the country. We piled into our Ford station wagon and drove toward Peggy's Cove Lighthouse, meandered around the picturesque Mahone Bay, or cruised through the Valley's apple orchards.

One Sunday, as I sat in my usual position by the driver's side back window, I realized Mum's voice had dropped to a whisper. I leaned forward and listened.

"I told my mother I'm pregnant again," Mum said.

Dad leaned toward her. "And what did she say?"

"Just what I expected." Sadness laced her tone. Mum patted her chest with a handkerchief, impersonating Nan. "Oh, me nerves. Don't-cha know when to quit?"

Dad snickered. "I promised to keep you barefoot and pregnant."

Mum wiped a tear from her cheek.

"It's not her problem," Dad said.

"I can't do this anymore, eh? This is the last one, mind you."

Their conversation ended as we turned into an A&W drive-in. Shortly after we ordered, the carhop hooked a serving tray on our car door. The aroma of grilled hamburgers, onion rings, and greasy fries filled our car. On her second trip, the waitress brought frosted mugs of delicious root beer.

Dad clicked on the radio. Between puffs on his cigarette, he blended his smooth baritone with that of his favorite country singer, Johnny Cash.

Marcus and I clicked mugs. "Cheers."

I inhaled a juicy cheeseburger and gulped down cold root beer. For the moment, life was good. Or so I thought.

A week later, I went with Dad across the bridge to Halifax. He held my hand as we entered a dilapidated apartment building and ascended a dimly lit stairwell.

"Where are we going?" I asked.

"To see my father."

"I didn't know I had a grandfather."

Dad knocked on apartment number nine. A poorly dressed woman ushered us into a musty bedroom and pulled back the curtains. The emaciated form of an older man lay with his face to the wall.

Dad pulled up a chair and gently rolled the man onto his back. "Dad, it's Dave," he said. My father put his arm around my waist and drew me close. "This is Susan, my daughter."

The man grunted.

"Kiss your grandfather," Dad said.

I pulled back as whisker-stubble prickled my lips. A fly buzzed around the room and landed on grandfather's hand. I grimaced. *Do I smell pee?*

Dad cleared his throat. "I can see you're not up for visitors. We'll leave you to rest."

A moment later, we descended the stairs to the car.

"What's wrong with Grandfather?"

"He's dying." Dad's voice was husky.

"How come we've never come here before?"

Dad brushed away a tear. "You ask too many questions."

On the way back to our apartment, I quietly watched out the window. Grandpa must have been a bad man. Why else would Dad have kept him a secret? And why else would we avoid visiting him?

Dave

Once again, he was showing up for work late and hungover. It wasn't the first time, but hopefully Dave's otherwise strong work ethic would lead his supervisor to continue overlooking the tardiness, as he'd been doing for years.

Dave approached the janitor's closet to find his supervisor waiting for him.

"I'm letting you go, buddy," the supervisor said.

"I'm sorry, I promise this won't happen again." He had to come up with a believable excuse, quick. "My car—"

"You reek of liquor." His boss stepped back, clearly repulsed.

"Wait. Please!" Dave begged. "I have a wife, five kids, and another one on the way."

His boss simply walked away.

Last Friday, he'd spent a large portion of his paycheck on alcohol. Now, that money was gone. In utter despair, Dave slid down the cold cinder block wall to the floor. With no dependable income, his family would face another eviction.

Two weeks later, he packed his family and all their worldly possessions into the back of their station wagon and drove to Toronto. He needed a fresh start, even if it would be 1800 miles away from his mother-in-law, his children's Grandma Nan.

CHAPTER SEVEN

Burst My Balloon

January 1970, Toronto, Ontario
Madeline

Madeline opened the silverware drawer and stepped back, allowing the hundred-plus roaches covering the utensils to retreat to safety. No can opener there. She jerked open another drawer.

I must have been crazy to marry at sixteen.

She finally found the worn-out, dull can opener and fumbled with a can of baked beans. The blade wouldn't catch.

Madeline slammed the beans down on the counter and surveyed the apartment. Although it was larger than any other place they'd lived, years of abuse had taken their toll. A glance out the window at East Queen Street reminded her that their neighborhood left much to be desired. The nearby, dilapidated buildings featured dirty pawn shops and a dozen dingy bars.

An ominous cloud of depression settled over her. At first Dave had found a new job. But once his employer learned he could barely read, he'd been fired. Dave spent what little money they had on beer and borrowed more they didn't have, to buy more beer. Delinquent bills lay open on the table, the kids constantly needed new clothes, and the electric company threatened to turn off the power. Would the pressure ever end?

She tried once more to open the can. Finally, the blade caught.

Madeline scraped the last bean into the saucepan. *I'm stuck in the ghettos, surrounded by snotty-nosed kids, and married to an illiterate loser.* She dashed away a tear.

Dave entered the kitchen and watched her add sliced hot dogs to the beans. "What did you do today, Maddie?"

"Ohhh, ya know, the usual. Dishes, laundry, *more* laundry. When the wringer on the washer isn't popping loose and actually *works*, I can't wring them out by hand, eh?"

She motioned to the pile of dirty clothes on the floor. Then she shuffled to the table and eased onto the cold metal chair. She propped her elbow on the table and rested her cheek on her hand. Madeline drummed her fingers on the warm teacup. "Frankly, I'm exhausted."

The wall clock ticked, ticked, ticked.

"And I don't care anymore," she said.

Dave filled a plate with beans and weenies and covered it with a blanket of salt. "Well, then you better just stay home."

"You're not hearing me." She let her resentment and bitterness flare. "I'm done with slaving around the house all day."

Dave scarfed down his meal and slammed the empty plate on the counter. "I'm going out for a drink."

"I'm not staying home while you make your daily trek to Harry's Den and hobnob with your buddies." She sprang up and stiffened her spine. Letting out her pent-up frustrations made her feel lighter, energized. She headed for the bedroom, calling back over her shoulder. "I'm going with you."

"What about the kids?" Dave asked.

A coldness washed through her. "They're old enough to fend for themselves."

Alone in her room, Madeline spritzed Lily of the Valley perfume on her neck and wrists. Her mirror reflected the glint of determination in her eyes. "The kids will be fine."

Summer 1970
Susan

Many mornings I found my parents battling a hangover while we readied ourselves for school. In the evenings, Mum and Dad spent their time either at the bar or out drinking with friends. Mum no longer cooked meals or kept up with the laundry.

I learned to pan-handle. Marcus and I often took turns standing at the bus stop begging for money. On a good day, in half an hour I might collect twenty-five cents, the cost of an order of fries with beef gravy. On weekends and after school, we frequented the local 7-Eleven. We learned to blend with the crowd and steal items that easily slid into our pockets or up our sleeves.

But we couldn't steal enough to meet our needs. And the morning pint of milk at school didn't benefit my toddler siblings at home.

One day, Marcus sat on the front steps throwing

pebbles at the phone booth. "We need money for groceries. And no more candy bars. It's not good for the babies."

"We should collect pop bottles," I said. "Each bottle is worth five cents."

From then on, Marcus and I searched everywhere for bottles. We checked the parks, ball fields, and smelly trashcans on our way to and from school. Marcus found a big cardboard box, and we hid it in the basement to use as a collection bin. When our container was full of bottles, Marcus asked his friend's brother to drive us to the store. We loaded the trunk of his car with our loot, grinning at our good fortune. We had worked hard to gather the pop bottles, and now our reward would be grocery money. As our helper cashed in the bottles, I stood in the corner of the IGA, drooling over the penny candy.

Marcus wandered over to stand beside me. "Okay. You can spend ten cents on sweets. The rest goes to groceries."

Our bottles earned us just over *twelve dollars*. When we arrived back home, we got out of the car, expecting the driver to give us the money. But he didn't offer.

"Hey, where's our money from the bottles?" Marcus asked.

The guy smirked. "Are you kidding? Your dad owes me fifty bucks for beer, and you owe me two for gas." He winked. "Let's just say we're even."

Marcus barged past me and ran into the house. I followed him to the kitchen and watched as he rummaged through the drawers.

"What are you looking for?" I asked.

"A pencil and some paper. I'm making a grocery list to show the manager at the IGA. If I sign Mum's name, they'll give us the food on credit."

I admired my brother's ingenuity. "You're so smart."

"Not really. I'm copying Mum." Marcus withdrew an old envelope and a broken pencil from the drawer. "We need to include some sensible things, like hot dogs and mac-n-cheese. If it's all cookies and chips, the manager will get suspicious."

For the next month, my brother and I purchased all our groceries on credit. Our scheme ended when the manager of IGA demanded payment on the loan.

I had to plan for that moment when hunger gripped my tummy. I found a sleeve of crackers and stashed it in the bottom drawer of my dresser.

October 1970

Mum's birthday was coming up, and I wanted to get her a special gift. But I didn't know what she wanted, and I had no money. Then I overheard her complain about the run in her stockings. That's what I'd get her—new stockings.

I targeted a row of shops on our street and offered to make food runs for the workers. I took their orders, then ran to the closest restaurant and fetched their meals or drinks. Each customer paid me a nickel for my service.

The day before Mum's birthday, I emptied my pockets and counted all the coins I'd earned. To my delight, I had just enough change to buy a pair of silk stockings.

I bubbled over with happiness, anticipating my mother's joy. I couldn't wait to see her face light up. I hoped to tiptoe from behind her and softly set the package in her lap—the perfect surprise. She might thank me and grace me with her I'm-pleased-with-you smile, the same look she gave

Marcus when he recited his multiplication tables.

In the kitchen with my gift in hand, I pushed a chair over to the refrigerator and climbed up. I could barely see the top.

Marcus entered the back door. "What are you doing?"

Puffs of dust scattered as I set down the package. "Hiding a birthday present for Mum."

"Nice. No one ever looks up there."

The special day arrived. I skipped into the kitchen to retrieve Mum's gift. Love for my mother pulsed through my veins.

A shiny spot, surrounded by dust bunnies, marked the place where the gift had been. But the package was gone.

I ran to the living room where Mum sat on the couch, watching a soap opera. "Mum, I had a gift for you on top of the fridge." My voice shook with threatening tears. "But now—"

"Oh, you mean the stockings I wore last night?" Her gaze stayed glued to the TV.

I pressed my hand over my mouth, choking on a sob.

Mum glanced up. "Don't cry, Suzie-Q. Marcus said they were from you." She winked and resumed watching her show.

My chin dropped to my chest, and I sprinted out the front door. *I should have hidden it somewhere else. Why hadn't I wrapped it? I should have bought perfume.*

I blinked back tears. My mother's impatience had denied me the joy of giving and the thrill of being appreciated. I sat on the rough curb and threw stones at passing streetcars. Deciding on the perfect gift, struggling to raise money, searching for the perfect hiding place, did all that effort count for nothing?

On the morning of my birthday, I found Mum preparing herself a cup of tea.

My birthday. I hope someone remembers.

"I have a surprise for you." Mum swirled boiling water in the teapot.

I gripped the edge of the metal table and bounced on my toes. "What is it?"

"If I told you, it wouldn't be a surprise now, would it?" Mum smoothed my hair. "Happy birthday, Do-Bee." She poured herself a cup of tea, added a heaping spoonful of sugar, a splash of milk.

The sun shone brightly through the kitchen window, as if giving a special glow to my special day. *Chirp, chirp.* Even the birds singing outside seemed to wish me a happy birthday. I hummed a merry tune as I followed Mum to the front porch.

By early afternoon, I smelled my birthday cake cooling in the kitchen. I rested my elbows on the table, leaning in to watch while Mum mixed powdered sugar and red food coloring. To my delight, she arranged nine, white daisy, candle holders in a circle around the edge of the cake.

"Can I have my surprise now?" I asked.

"Oh, alright." She opened the cupboard, reached to the back of the second shelf, and pulled out a bag of oversized balloons. I loved everything about the balloons— the bright colors, the laughter they would bring, and especially the fact that they were for me.

"These are not ordinary balloons. They're giant," Mum said.

I didn't know of anyone else lucky enough to have a whole bag of *those* for their birthday. I threw my arms around her waist. "What a day! Thanks, Mum."

"I told your Aunt I'd send you to fetch your cousins while we blow up the balloons. Here's change to pay your fare."

I calculated the time it would take to fetch my cousins. A minimum of three hours. Would my siblings be willing to wait that long? I worried they wouldn't. "But Mum, I'll be gone all afternoon."

"It will take your brother all afternoon to blow up these balloons."

Polly, Marcus, and his friend from upstairs came in the back door. Mum tossed the bag of balloons to Marcus. "Here you go, kids. Start working on these."

"This will take forever," Marcus complained.

I hurried out. After a five-minute wait at the bus stop, I caught the downtown streetcar and rode twenty minutes to the opposite end of Queen Street. I arrived at my aunt's apartment and entered without knocking.

"Hi there, birthday girl. Did you like your present?" Aunt Edith resumed her phone conversation without waiting for my answer. I often thought the phone had become part of her ear. I never saw her without it.

"Where are my cousins?" I asked.

Aunt Edith placed her hand over the receiver. "Outside playing, but I told them to be back in an hour. Why don't you watch TV?"

I followed my aunt's instructions. I only found sports on the TV. Saturday afternoon programs were always boring. I resigned myself to a long wait and nestled into the couch.

My cousins returned later that afternoon, and we rode the streetcar to my house. I was smiling so big my face hurt. This was my special day. I was going to have a party with guests and everything, for *my* birthday!

I found Mum and her girlfriend sitting on the sofa gossiping and joking. A million, multi-colored balloon bits littered the living room floor. A tingling numbness surged through my body.

"You missed the party," Mum said without looking up. She waved her hand toward the mess.

My vision blurred with unshed tears.

"Now, now, don't cry! I had them save you one. It's over there." She motioned to an end table.

Immediately, my cousins dove for the balloon, smashing it against the wall. The *pop!* echoed through the room, and my cousins laughed gleefully at the noise.

I trembled with anger. *Brats.*

"There's cake in the kitchen," Mum said.

My excitement over my special day and all my desire to celebrate left me. With heavy steps, I sulked my way to the kitchen. My cousins beat me there and helped themselves to pieces of my already half-eaten cake, then went out the back door to play.

Alone, I served myself a slice of birthday cake. It tasted like sawdust. Neither as sweet nor as enjoyable as I had imagined it would be.

No candles.

No song.

No gifts.

My throat tightened with anguish, making swallowing difficult. I thought my heart would break into a thousand pieces.

I cut a second piece of cake, licked off the icing, and wrapped it in a napkin. I tucked it in my pocket and slipped into my bedroom. Then I pulled back the clothes in my bottom dresser drawer and, ever so gently, placed the tiny provision beside a can of mustard sardines and a wad of "ABC" (already-been-chewed) bubble gum.

With my back pressed against the wall, I slumped to the floor. Then I pulled my knees to my chest and buried my face in the crook of my arm. *Happy Birthday to me.* I rocked and wept, releasing my sorrow in a flood of hot tears.

CHAPTER EIGHT

Merry Christmas

December 1970
Susan

Before that Christmas season, the only Christmas songs I knew were "Rudolph the Red-Nosed Reindeer" and "Here Comes Santa Claus." Then my school began playing Christmas carols over the intercom for the first five minutes of each day. I intently listened to "Silent Night" and "O Little Town of Bethlehem." When I heard "Angels We Have Heard on High," I wondered why angels sang for the shepherds. "Away in a Manger" brought to mind the life-size figures I had seen outside a local church.

One day during my lunch break, I stopped by the church to examine the creche with its figures: a woman, a man, a baby, farm animals, and a bright angel holding a star. What did this family have to do with Christmas?

The year before, I had attended my sister's Christmas Program, *Charlie Brown's Christmas*. At least he had a tree. By the look of things in the manger, baby Jesus had nothing but straw and a blue blanket.

Shortly thereafter, Dad warned us Grandma Goldie

was going to visit and told us to be on our best behavior. The day she came, I sat erect and still on the couch with Marcus, Polly, and Davie. Grandma Goldie sat across from us, smelling like a giant box of talcum powder.

"Who wants to be the first one to say a memory verse?" she encouraged, offering us a lollipop as a reward.

My eyes widened. "What's a memory verse?"

Grandma covered her mouth with her hand and chuckled. "Such an amusing child."

None of us laughed.

"I'm talking about Scriptures from the Bible," Grandma said with a cough.

We stared at her.

"Okay, let's try a song. Can you sing a chorus you learned in Sunday school?"

None of us moved.

Grandma leaned forward and hummed a tune.

I exchanged glances with my siblings and shrugged.

"Honestly, Dave, your children are downright heathen." Grandma scowled.

The following Sunday, Dad sent us to church, each of us with a nickel in our pocket.

We sang the chorus "No, You Can't Get to Heaven Without S-A-L-V-A-T-I-O-N." I'd never scored a perfect mark in spelling, ever. Learning to spell long words? Totally out of the question. But while singing the song, I was spelling a long word. S-a-l-v-a-t-i-o-n.

In Sunday school, I leaned forward and listened to the Bible story. Three wise men from the desert hopped on their camels and took a long journey to deliver birthday gifts to Jesus. That made me glad. Now, Jesus' parents would have something to sell at the pawnshop and get money to move out of the barn.

Throughout the service, we each fingered the nickels in our pockets. When the offering plate came our way, Marcus shook his head. I winked and patted my coat pocket. On the way home, we spent our change on penny candy.

A couple weeks later, I attended another church with Marcus. A friendly lady met us at the front door and led us to our age-appropriate classes. After Sunday school, I stood in the vestibule, waiting for my brother. Two large wooden doors adorned with leaded glass windows muffled the sound of angelic music on the other side. A free show!

When a gentleman exited, leaving the doors swinging behind him, I slipped through into the auditorium.

The beauty that surrounded me took my breath away. Antique lights swung gracefully on long black chains suspended from a cathedral ceiling. As I tiptoed on the plush red carpet in the center aisle, multi-colored rays from the stained-glass windows swirled on my clothing. I chose a seat on a cushioned bench, three rows from the back.

I closed my eyes, leaning back against the pew, and soaked in the soothing blend of notes pouring from the organ in a song of the season. I chuckled to myself. *Here come the sheep and the camels, shuffling along the dirt path to the village.* Warm tones of two violins and a classical guitar joined the organ. *Ahh, this is the heavenly music of the angels.* I'd never heard anything so glorious. Cheerful notes from a silver flute danced higher and higher above the piano melody. *Now the angels are flying back and forth to the stars —*

Someone tapped my shoulder.

"This service is only for adults," my Sunday school teacher said with authority. She motioned for me to leave. "Now run along."

Disapproving glances from the audience and embarrassment cloaked me as Miss Grouch escorted me out.

Television shows provided the only magic of Christmas in our home. During Christmas break, I stayed up late every night watching Christmas-themed romance movies. I marveled at the houses filled with fancy decorations, mounds of beautifully wrapped presents, and platters of iced sugar cookies. Sitting on the sofa with only the glow of the television, I imagined myself as the little girl who received her happy ending.

In reality, our apartment remained void of anything seasonal. There were no Christmas decorations, no gifts, and no holiday foods. Mum and Dad spent all their time at the bar drowning their holiday blues with cheap whiskey and cold beer.

My siblings and I huddled in our heatless apartment on Christmas morning. Neither Mum nor Dad had returned home the night before. Davie, Thomas, and Polly sat on the couch, looking forlorn.

"What's with you?" I asked.

Polly sniffed. "Why didn't Santa come to our house?"

I had been wondering the same thing. I snuggled in beside my siblings and put my arm around Thomas. "I'm afraid Santa and Rudolph aren't real. They're pretend, just like fairies and leprechauns." I'm pretty sure that made us all feel worse.

"Susan, put on your coat and come with me," Marcus said. "Polly, stay here with the babies."

"My sneakers are still sopping wet from yesterday," I said.

Marcus reached for the door. "You wanna eat?"

Dressed in knit hats and coats with broken zippers, we ventured outside. I shoved my hands deep into my pockets and curled my fingers into fists. To avoid the icy sidewalks, we climbed over a mound of dirty snow and walked in the deserted street. All the stores along Queen Street were closed. Even the occasional streetcar lacked passengers. I wouldn't be able to steal or beg today.

Marcus led us to the foyer of an apartment building. "My hands are freezing," he said.

He warmed himself by the register while I removed my shoes and rubbed my frozen feet. Warm blood circulated into my toes, accompanied by a prickly, tingling sensation. I pulled my feet back through the holes in my leotards and folded the stockings over my toes. Ever so carefully, I slid my feet back into my sneakers.

We returned home empty-handed.

"I have something we can eat," I said.

Marcus herded our siblings into the kitchen while I collected my secret food stash items. Huddled around the table, we shared a meager Christmas dinner of canned sardines and a sleeve of saltine crackers.

My sister, Polly, spent most of her after-school hours and most of Christmas break at a friend's house, playing with fancy toys and eating nutritious meals. Because of her frequent visits, her friend's parents called Polly their adopted daughter.

One evening as my brothers and I built a tower with blocks, Polly arrived home and paused to watch us. The aroma of roast beef lingered on her clothing.

Polly kicked at the tower. "Where's Mum and Dad?"

I swatted her leg but didn't look up. "At the bar."

"Can I walk down there and tell them goodnight?"

I rolled my eyes. "No, silly, you can't go in there."

"Why not?"

"Because it's adults only."

"I want to show them the Christmas gifts from my friends."

I glanced at her stylish navy and green wool jacket and the matching checkered scarf. Genuine happiness for my sister's good fortune rose within me. How wonderful for her.

"They have a coat for you, too," she said.

Gratitude washed over me. I turned away to hide the tears pooling in my eyes.

"It's brown with white lines on the pockets and around the hood," Polly continued. "I told them you'd love it."

I blushed at the thought of the ragged coat I'd been forced to wear for so long. The generosity of my sister's friend brightened my world. I wanted to express my gratitude but struggled to swallow the lump in my throat.

Polly twirled her elegant scarf. "Will Dad come home sick and throwing up?"

The night before, Dad had spewed vomit the entire length of the hallway, splattering the walls and floor. Then he proceeded to the washroom and threw up more in the tub.

I groaned. "I hope not."

Polly stood still, hesitating to enter the hallway. "Did anyone clean?" She gagged.

I nodded.

Tears shimmered in her hazel eyes. I squirmed, embarrassed by my sister's expression of thanks, then shooed her away with a flick of my hand.

Days after Christmas, my siblings and I answered a knock at the front door and found a worker from a local charity loaded with packages. He presented each of us with a box wrapped in beautiful gold paper containing candy, a toy, and an article of clothing. Polly and I were thrilled to receive matching red and gray striped sweaters. One piece of clothing—that's all we needed to participate in the traditional "What did you receive for Christmas?" show and tell at school.

The first day back, I waited for Polly in the hallway after school. "Every poor kid wore the same sweater," I said when she drew near.

Polly brushed away a tear. "Yes. I saw stripes everywhere. T-totally embarrassing." She sniffed and wiped her nose on her sleeve. "I will never, ever again wear this sweater."

As soon as we got home, I threw my striped sweater in the trash. I refused to broadcast my poverty.

Susan Carter

CHAPTER NINE

Darkness

July 1971, East Queen Street
Susan

At nine years old, dread was my constant companion. Home alone each night as the evening shadows lengthened, I curled up on the tattered sofa in the front room of our apartment. And when the living room's colors faded to an indistinguishable gray, I hurried to my room, searching for light. My stash of matches I kept for nights like this had dwindled. I withdrew the last candle and pressed the flat bottom into a pool of melted wax on a saucer, a procedure I had followed the previous three evenings.

The clock's ticking seemed to grow louder as the measured seconds pulsed with flickering candlelight in the deepening darkness. As the candle burned lower and lower, the weight in my chest increased. When the flame extinguished, I would face a greater terror—rats. When less than a half-inch of candle remained, I summoned my last ounce of courage and rose to check on my siblings.

I tiptoed to the door of the first bedroom, the size of a walk-in closet, and peered into the darkness. A wooden crib stood alone in the otherwise empty room. In daylight, a curtain-less window behind the bed revealed the forest green wall of the building next door. At night, not even the faintest light penetrated this dungeon-like room.

At fourteen months old, Aulden spent his days in solitude, trapped there in his crib. He had not yet mastered the art of climbing out. Aulden's constant cries usually went unnoticed as they blended with the roar of traffic from Queen Street. Occasionally, when I remembered to check on him, I found him standing at the side of his crib, his face shining with a sticky, watery mixture of tears and snot.

Pitiful.

Every time I looked into his haunting dark eyes a sharp pain gouged my conscience. He would reach out with both hands, palms up, his glassy stare begging me to rescue him. But Mum had said crying developed an infant's lungs. So, I forced myself to look away, believing babies belonged in their cribs.

That evening, I cracked open his door and heard him moaning softly in his sleep. His little hands clung to the wooden spindles of the crib. I stepped back, repulsed by the overwhelming stench of urine and stinky diaper. A wave of guilt washed over me as I thought of the many hours the baby had endured in this depressing hole.

I closed his door and hurried on to the next bedroom. A rickety bunk bed leaned against the far wall. Marcus had claimed the top bunk, but he slept at his friend's house most nights. My brother Davie lay on the bottom bunk he usually shared with Thomas. But for the last month, Davie had slept alone. Thomas remained in the hospital, healing from a broken leg.

I remembered the night Marcus had come home, his face ashen white.

My voice had choked with fear. "What happened?"

"I took Davie and Thomas for a ride on the streetcar," Marcus said. "I held hands with both of them. But at the stoplight, Thomas saw the beach. He jerked free and ran onto the highway."

I gasped.

"A guy driving a pickup swerved, and his trailer caught Thomas by his jeans and drug him twenty feet." Marcus covered his face and sobbed.

"Is, is he—" I shuddered at the unthinkable.

"He broke his leg, and I'm not sure what else." Marcus sat on the sofa and wiped his nose on his sleeve.

"They took him to the hospital?"

"Yeah, but I don't know which one." Marcus scrubbed his eyes. "How will Mum and Dad find him?"

I shrugged.

"Is Mum home?"

Mum had disappeared three days prior, following a fistfight with Dad. "I haven't seen her," I said.

After being in the hospital for six weeks, Thomas finally returned home. One day, I placed him, cast and all, in the stroller. I instructed Davie to balance himself on the bar connecting the rear wheels. And off we set for a walk to our favorite destination, the City Hall fountain.

Thomas called out directions to Davie. "Bump ahead. Red light. Here comes a dog." We reached the fountain and sat on the steel bench at the plaza, cheering for the passers-by who threw treats to the pigeons.

Another day, I tried to bring along baby Aulden, but that proved disastrous. I struggled to manipulate the carriage with one hand while holding onto Davie with the other. Exhaustion set in by the end of the fifth block, and the joy of the outing evaporated. I simply couldn't handle all three of them at once. So the next time, I left Aulden at home and swallowed the guilt of leaving him behind.

One week after Thomas came home from the hospital, he sat on the floor, whimpering, as I changed channels on the television.

"Ooh, my leg hurts," he said.

A rancorous odor seeped from the cast. "Smells like you need a bath, but I can't get the plaster wet," I said.

His cries escalated into wails that turned his face beet red.

His groaning ripped my heart, but I continued watching TV. What help could I offer? "Nothing I can do, buddy."

The next moment, Thomas lay on the floor, dead silent, his skin turning blue. I clutched at my chest. "Oh, God, what's happening?"

A moment later, the front door flew open. Dad's sister, my Aunt Sharon, surprised me by rushing inside.

"Where's your father?" She looked upset, but I didn't know about what.

"Working," I said.

"Your mum?"

"Haven't seen her."

She motioned toward Thomas. "What's wrong with him?"

I smeared tears across my cheeks. "I don't know."

Aunt Sharon picked up Thomas, jabbed her finger down his throat, and dug out his tongue. Thomas gasped for air.

"He'll be okay now," she said. Since Dad wasn't home, she left.

The moment Dad arrived home, I mentioned the foul odor coming from Thomas' cast. Dad called a taxi to take Thomas to the hospital.

The concern on my dad's face told me Thomas was in bad shape. As I watched the taxi merge into traffic, I felt so alone. If only Mum were home. Where was she? I was sure she would want to know about Thomas needing to go back to the hospital.

That same night as I made my way to the last bedroom, the one I shared with my sister, my candle sputtered. Tonight, Polly had the bed all to herself. I would be sleeping on the sofa in the living room. Since Polly had taken a friend's advice of pushing miniature marshmallows into her ears, the noise of the rats ceased to bother her. She lay wrapped in Dad's wool jacket, her head flat on the threadbare sheet covering a lumpy mattress.

She rolled over and moaned. "Psychedelic hamburgers."

I smirked. My sister's nighttime babbles constantly amused me.

Bang! Bang! Someone was pounding on the front door. I ran back to the living room, my candle dripping wax. Three sets of locks secured our door: two barrel bolts, two chains, and two deadbolts.

From the apartment building foyer, a male voice shouted slurred obscenities.

Why was a drunken man trying to break into our

apartment? Who was he?

He struck the door again; it shook on the hinges.

I retreated to the sofa and sucked my knuckle. The drunk groaned and repeatedly slammed his body against the door. One by one, the locks fell to the floor, leaving only the deadbolts holding the door in place. I squirmed as the door frame caved several inches.

A knot formed in the pit of my stomach. Was I safer down the hall with the rats, or should I stay put and face a drunken maniac? I considered the risk. My memory flashed back to the Dartmouth dentist, and a chill ran down my spine. I might be better off with the rodents.

Frantic, I scanned the room for a safe hiding place. My candle flickered and died, plunging the room into darkness.

I froze.

The intruder lunged at the door again, pushing it farther in. I held my breath. One more push, and he would be inside with me.

Wham! The man cursed and kicked the wall beside our door. But the frame held. Mercifully, a moment later, he gave up and stumbled into the night.

I squeezed my trembling hands together in relief. Then, squeaking came from inside the basement door.

Rats.

Like an advancing army, the rodents made their ascent. The size of cats with whip-like tails, the rats hid in the basement shadows during daylight and took over the apartment as soon as darkness fell. They ran all over the house, jumping on the beds and on us. They scurried down the hall, their nails scratching the floorboards, carrying their treasures from the kitchen back to their nests in the ductwork. They often slammed into the basement door with loud thuds.

Sitting alone in the dark, I strained at every sound. The clacking of an approaching streetcar grew louder, then faded as it lumbered past—eleven o'clock. The last streetcar of the evening.

I cried for my Nan's loving embrace. If she were there, she would rescue me from the darkness, the drunk, and the rats. I closed my eyes and imagined the Public Gardens of Halifax, graceful swans on the pond, and Nan, sitting beside me on the park bench. Eventually, I drifted to sleep.

I don't know how long I slept—not very long, I'm sure. The jangling of the public phone from the booth in front of our apartment startled me awake. Since it served as the only line of communication for our building, I felt pressured to answer. Groggy from sleep, I entered the foyer and peeked out the front door.

A homeless man named Mike drew near, staggering toward the shelter in the next block. He banged his head on each telephone pole as he progressed toward his destination. "The spirits are after me! Here they come!" His eyes rolled back as he screamed, then ran to the next pole.

To avoid Mike, I hid behind the front door. After he passed, I sprinted to the phone booth, hoping the ringing would stop before I reached it. The thought of knocking on a neighbor's door at midnight, even to give a message, terrified me. But I knew I might not remember to deliver a message to anyone the following day.

Ring. Ring. Ring.

"Hello?" I gripped the cold phone with my sweaty hand.

"Is this Madeline?" asked a woman.

My curiosity piqued. "This is her daughter."

"Put your mother on the line."

"I can get my dad."

"Fine."

"I'm answering from a public phone. Give me a moment to find—"

"This is the nurse from Children's Hospital. Tell your father your brother needs emergency surgery, and we need his verbal permission to operate."

I stared into the night in the direction of the bar my dad frequented, unsure of what to do.

"Are you listening to me?" Her voice rose several decibels.

"Yes. I have to find Dad first."

I wished my father would appear, breaking through the darkness, stepping into the beam of light streaming from the phone booth. With my hand over the receiver, I squeezed my eyes shut and crossed my fingers. For added effect, I crossed my ankles. "Send Dad home right now." My words bounced off the Plexiglas and back into my face.

I waited. One. Two. Three seconds. Nothing happened.

What should I do? Should I mention the bar?

Reaching the tavern, locating my father then returning would take several minutes. In the meantime, my brother might die.

Would I be betraying Dad if I tell the lady he's drunk and unable to take her call?

"I'll wait." The nurse's stern voice pushed me to action.

I left the receiver dangling from the frayed cord and banging against the side of the booth, then turned toward the bar. I opened the folding door with my elbow and stepped timidly into the darkness. *Forget walking.* I broke into a run.

I thought back to the night Marcus had warned me not to walk the streets after dark.

"Who cares where I walk?" I'd asked. "I've traveled from one end of Queens to the other at night. Alone." I nodded for emphasis, feigning courage.

At first, Marcus didn't answer. Then he placed his arm around my shoulder and pointed to the boys standing in a doorway across the street. "Any idea why they're blowing up a paper bag?"

I shook my head.

"They're sniffing glue." Marcus squeezed my arm. "Don't mess with them, or they'll hurt you."

But this was an emergency. What choice did I have but to pass the glue-sniffers?

Fear coursed through my veins like jet fuel. I raced past the fume-filled doorway, my feet barely touching the ground, leaving the glue-sniffers and the pungent odor of adhesive in my wake.

I arrived at Harry's Den and pushed on the carved door. It didn't budge. There had to be another entrance, perhaps a back door. My imagination ran wild with what might be lurking in the shadows of the alley.

Then the barroom door creaked open, and a wrinkled man with a sullen face staggered past me. I grabbed the door before it closed and peeked into the saloon. The inky blackness of the taproom appeared ten times more intense than the darkness of the night. Neon lights highlighted an assortment of liquors and revealed the haze of smoke filling the room. A melancholy version of "Evil Grows in the Dark" blared from the jukebox, overpowering a cacophony of drunken voices and tinkling glasses.

I stepped back and wrung my hands. Once my eyes adjusted to the dimness, I could go booth by booth searching for Dad.

But what if I had to explain myself at each table? I shuddered. With their inebriated brains, the patrons wouldn't comprehend the urgency of my message. I could lose precious minutes trying to make them understand. Or worse, would Dad be embarrassed when his friends realized he had left his children unsupervised? I imagined him staggering home and cursing the nurse for interrupting his evening.

I planted my heel on the threshold, preventing the door from closing behind me and trapping me in the saloon. The joint reeked of nicotine and alcohol. Boisterous guffaws swelled in the booth closest to the exit. What a party!

Instinct warned me not to waste precious time in indecision. Thomas needed help right then. Anger surged deep within me. If my parents were home where they belonged, they wouldn't have missed a call from the hospital.

I fled the tavern and hurried back to the phone. As I ran, my anger intensified, dispelling any fear of the night or the glue-sniffers. Breathless and half choking, I reached the booth and grabbed the dangling receiver. To my surprise, the nurse remained on the line.

I pressed my hand to my trembling lips. "My dad's out drinking, and my mum's not here."

"Mercy! You're home alone?"

I brushed away a tear. "Yes."

"Hmm. I'm filing a formal complaint of neglect. We'll

proceed with the surgery."

I exhaled with relief. My brother would be okay. Undoubtedly, the nurse would send the police to kick my parents in the seat of the pants.

I stayed on the line, hoping for a few words of comfort, expecting a "good night."

Instead, she hung up, and the hum of a disconnected line, the sound of rejection, mocked my fears.

Susan Carter

CHAPTER TEN

The Secret

August 1971
Susan

I was out by the street when I heard the shouting from the house. I ran inside to discover Mum crouched in the corner of the bedroom, one arm covered her head and the other wrapped defensively around her torso.

"Maddie, I *saw* you look at him!" Dad said.

The intensity and volume of Dad's voice shocked me.

"Why did you move over and make room for him to sit at our table?" Dad continued.

"He pushed his way in beside me," Mum said.

Dad's knuckles whitened as he tightened his hand into a fist.

I knew Dad regularly hit Mum. I had seen her bruises and heard her relate the stories to my aunt. But I had never witnessed their fights.

Mum's face distorted with fear. "Don't hit me, Dave. Don't hit me."

I covered my mouth and suppressed a scream.

Dad cursed and smashed his fist into the plaster wall,

inches above Mum.

Later that day, Mum and I returned from visiting Aunt Edith. As we disembarked the streetcar, Mum grabbed my arm and turned me to face her. "Your father and I will be splitting up."

I sucked in a gulp of air and held it. "Are we staying with you?" I crossed my fingers. *Don't make me choose which parent I love most. That's unthinkable.*

"I will keep you girls and leave the boys with your father." Mum smiled at me in a half-reassuring, half-apologetic way.

Live separated from my brothers? My world spun out of focus. Who would care for them? How would I find their new home? Without Marcus, I'd have no sense of security at all.

"I gave up a child once," Mum said. "Rose. Her name is Rose. Every year on her birthday, I think of her." She gazed off as if seeing something I couldn't, then inhaled sharply. "Yep," she whispered.

What was Mum saying? Did I have another sister? I'd never heard of her. And, Rose ... what a beautiful name!

I froze, letting the startling truth sink into my soul. My mother gave away her baby? How was that possible?

"Don't worry. I won't repeat that mistake," Mum said.

I remembered the twins, Coleen and Claire, and how my relatives had kept their adoption a secret. But I couldn't recall my parents fighting for my sisters. Coleen, Claire, and now Rose. Would I be next?

I held my tummy, nauseated from this glimpse at the darker side of my mother. *How do parents walk away from their children? How could a mother?*

"When are we leaving?" I fell in step beside Mum.

"I don't know," Mum said with a nervous titter. "I need to find a boyfriend first, right?"

I didn't see or recognize the humor in her words.

A car honked as it passed. Mum spun toward the driver and winked at him.

I cringed. Would I find that man knocking at our door? How long before Mum left again? I worried that this time she would not return. But what if Dad took my brothers? If only I were dreaming and could simply wake up from the nightmare.

A few days later, I went home on my school lunch break. I had just enough time to grab a peanut butter sandwich and get back to class. As I made my way to the kitchen, I heard loud voices coming from the back porch.

I stepped onto the porch, letting the screen door bang behind me. Mum sat on the top step, smiling, and talking with a strange man.

"What's going on, Suzie-Q?" Mum asked. "This is Susan, my second child."

The stranger winked. "Hey there, cutie."

I blinked. *Don't even tell me your name, Mr. Ugly. I couldn't care less.*

"You'd better go back to school," Mum said. "Or you'll be late for afternoon classes, right?"

I retreated inside, weighed down by despair. Mum was serious about leaving Dad. This was bad. Really bad.

The front door squeaked open just as I was about to leave.

"Where's your mother?" Dad scowled. He stank of

alcohol.

If he discovered Mum was flirting … "I, I don't know."

Fury flashed in his eyes. "Trying to protect her, are you?"

He smacked me. I flew backward, slamming against the wall, my cheek stinging. I landed on the floor with a thud in a crumpled heap.

"I can tell when you're lying." Dad staggered down the hall, stumbling into one wall, then the other.

He's angry enough to kill Mum. Numb with concern for her, I cried out to God. *Protect my Mum.*

The back door slammed. "Maddie, where are you?" Dad yelled.

I started breathing again. Mum had escaped. Fearing another encounter with my father's wrath, I hurried out the front door and returned to school.

Neither of my parents returned home that night. I figured Mum had run away again. But the following morning, I overheard my father talking with Marcus in the kitchen. "Your mother and I are taking the train to British Columbia. Take this dime. If we're not back in three days, call the police. Tell them you are home alone. They will send someone to help you."

Later, I stood on the sidewalk with my brother, waving goodbye. Dad gripped Mum's elbow and guided her onto the streetcar. We watched the traffic until the streetcar disappeared.

For the next three days, when I returned home from school I wandered through the house, searching in vain for my parents. I was sure they would return like all the times before. But their bed remained untouched. Empty. Mum and Dad didn't come back.

We had no food, no electricity, and no income. We needed help. But calling the police was a last resort.

As Marcus and I discussed a survival plan, I pressed my fingertips to my temples, my brain throbbing with the overload of possibilities, unanswered questions, and unknowns.

"We can go live with one of our grandmothers in Nova Scotia," I said.

"No. Where would we get money for the train? Besides, Grandma is sick," Marcus said of Dad's mum. "She can barely take care of herself."

"And how do you know?"

"I overheard Dad talking."

"What about Nan?"

Marcus rolled his eyes. "Again, tickets? Besides, Nan is already raising Aunt Edith's three boys. Her beds are full."

Crunch. I stomped on a roach and felt no sympathy.

There I was with my five siblings. We were alone in the world, without food, without a plan.

Completely abandoned.

Susan Carter

CHAPTER ELEVEN

Emergency Shelter

August 1971
Susan

While Marcus called the police, I waited with Polly outside the phone booth. He hung up and joined us.

I sucked in my breath. "Why did you do that?" I knew why, but I hadn't wanted him to do it.

"Dad said the police would find us a place to stay while he and Mum are away."

Polly crossed her arms and shot out her lower lip. "I'll ask my friend's mum to adopt me."

Marcus turned to leave. "Call me when the cops arrive. I'm going upstairs to tell my friends goodbye."

"I'm going, too," Polly said.

"I'm scared," I said, but neither of them seemed to hear me.

I entered the apartment and found four-year-old Davie on the sofa. "The police are coming." I didn't want to scare him, so I used a gentle tone. "They might ask us where our parents are and why they left." I stared at the floor, shaking my head. "I don't know what to say."

Davie's eyes filled, and his lower lip quivered. "Are we going to jail?"

"No." I gave him a shaky smile. "You and Aulden hide in the closet, so you won't have to talk to them. Okay?"

Pit-a-pat, pit-a-pat. Davie's bare feet sounded on the floor as he followed me to Aulden's room. He waited as I lifted the baby out of his crib and sniffed his diaper. I didn't have time to change it right then. I led them to the closet in Davie's room and dug a nest for them in a mound of dirty clothes.

I held my finger to my lips. "Shh, be quiet. I promise to come back for you."

Davie nodded, tears spilling down his cheeks. Aulden quietly studied Davie's face, his lip quivering in empathy. When I shut the door, both boys wailed.

Outside, a siren screamed. The red and blue flashing lights of a police car strobed on the walls of our living room. My mouth went so dry my tongue stuck to the roof. I lifted the curtain and peeked out the window. The policeman stood on the sidewalk talking with a nicely dressed woman. He pointed toward our apartment.

A moment later, the woman entered our home without knocking. She lifted a handkerchief to her nose and surveyed the front room.

"I'm the social worker from Children's Services." She glared at everything—the tattered furniture, the dingy walls, the dirty floors.

I trailed behind her as she followed the wails and eventually opened the closet door. Perhaps the mountain of dirty clothes ticked her off, or maybe she was simply an angry person. At any rate, she whirled on me and planted her free hand on her hip. "Where are the other children?"

"One of my brothers is in the hospital, one is upstairs,

and my sister is next door." *Who did she think she was coming in here and ordering me around?*

"Fetch your brothers something to eat!" She demanded.

"They're not hungry." I refused to tell her we had no food. Let her discover that for herself.

She pursed her lips and marched toward the kitchen. My cheeks burned with humiliation as I thought of the limp carrot and half a can of beer she would find in the icebox.

A moment later, she returned to the living room, fished in her purse, and held out a dollar to me. "Go to the restaurant across the street and buy a couple orders of fries with gravy." Her voice held a hint of compassion.

I didn't like this woman, and I certainly didn't want her pity. But my brothers were hungry. And the thought of fries and beef gravy made my mouth water. I snatched the money and headed for the café.

An hour later, the social worker loaded us into her station wagon and drove to the ritzy section of town. Her car slowed and took a left onto a drive lined with red maples. Between the branches, a two-story pink mansion with forest green shutters greeted us.

"This is an emergency shelter," the social worker said. "You will be here a few days until Children's Services makes other arrangements." She pulled to a stop, and we tumbled out onto the drive.

Polly leaned against the car, earnestly sucking her thumb.

I slapped her hand. "You'll get buck teeth."

Ignoring my warning, Polly blinked twice and turned toward the house.

I held onto Davie and guided him past the alternating gold and burgundy mums lining the path. Then we all reached a posh living room and sat. I eavesdropped on the social worker explaining our situation and discussing our care with the hostess of the shelter.

A sudden movement caught my attention. A terrier, obviously used to living and roaming inside the home, entered the room and stared at me. I stiffened. Once, a rabid dog had bitten Polly, and my parents rushed her to the clinic for shots.

More recently, when Thomas had returned from the hospital, we gave him a stray puppy as a welcome home gift. Mud covered that dog from the tip of his nose to the end of his tail. We wrangled him into the tub and doused him with dish soap and warm water. To our chagrin, a million fleas surged to the surface, giving the pup's fur a life of its own. The fleas jumped on the tub walls and crawled up our arms. Marcus and I screamed and ran outside, the pup scrambling after us. He disappeared, covered in flea-speckled suds, and never returned.

In general, canines terrified me. I wiped my sweaty palms on my jeans. A pounding came in my ears, drowning out the adult voices. My world shrank to the dog and what he might do next.

The terrier slowly made his way to my side. His eyes shone with kindness, and his tail gently wagged. An angel must have laid a hand on me and quieted my fears. I sat perfectly still while the dog licked the sour pus from the open sore on my leg. His tongue scrubbed the wound until it stung, but it immediately started feeling better.

"These kids are hungry," the social worker said.

"They need something to eat."

I followed the hostess into a formal dining room.

"You may help." She handed me fine china plates imprinted with tiny roses.

I carefully set the table, admiring the crystal chandelier sparkling above us and the rose-colored, velvet drapes dressing the windows. The house was so fancy, and I hoped I didn't break anything. My tummy rumbled. What would the lady fix for us to eat? Maybe she'd cook a gourmet something-or-other.

I stepped outside and called to Marcus and Polly. "Hey, guys, come quick. You should see the dining room. I helped set the table."

"What's for lunch?" Polly asked.

"I hope it's not beans and weenies," I said.

We laughed and ran to the house, anticipating a home-cooked meal. To our chagrin, one, solitary Twinkie occupied the center of each plate. I didn't want sweets. I wanted real food.

Seeing our surprise, the hostess grew defensive. "It's a mid-afternoon snack. We'll have a full meal at the proper time."

"When?" Polly quickly retorted.

Our hostess responded with an arrogant tilt of her chin. Finally, in the early evening, we sat down to a meal of hot beef stew and rolls. I ate like a starved wolf and cleaned every last bite on my plate.

Two days later, the social worker gathered Marcus, Davie, Polly, and me in the living room. "You are being placed with an elderly lady named Mrs. Jenkins. You will go there tomorrow. Davie, when the doctor releases Thomas from the hospital, you and your brother will be placed with a different foster family. Aulden will go to an orphanage for children under the age of two."

Later that evening, as my siblings and I prepared for bed, I thought of Aulden alone and without family. The more I visualized Aulden's isolation, the more despondent I felt. "What do you think the orphanage is like?" I asked Marcus.

"Well, I don't think this is a true story, but every day right before recess, our teacher reads a chapter from *Anne of Green Gables*," Marcus said. "Anne was an orphan from Nova Scotia. The book talks about her time in an orphanage."

"What does it say?"

"In Anne's orphanage, the bedroom walls were lined with beds. I think a dozen kids shared one room."

I crossed my fingers. "Well, at least Aulden won't be lonely."

The next morning at 8:30, we looked out the window to see a new social worker parked in the emergency shelter driveway.

I stood at the front door holding Aulden. Polly stood next to me, sucking her thumb of one hand while twirling her hair with the other. Marcus was next to her, his arm around Davie's shoulder. We all waited while the woman made her way up the front steps.

Her kind blue eyes sparkled as she greeted us. "Good morning, children. My name is Linda."

We stepped aside to let her pass.

She spoke briefly with the emergency shelter hostess then turned back to us. "We'd better get going, kids. Your foster mum is waiting."

Since we had no luggage, we had no excuse to stall. Marcus, Polly, and I gave Davie and Aulden one last tearful kiss.

As we pulled away, I turned around to see Davie and Aulden standing in the doorway, appearing forlorn and forsaken. I pressed my face to the cold window. Tears blurred my vision and coursed down my cheeks. Would my brothers be okay?

They think we're abandoning them. What could I do to stop this?

I dug my fingers into my hair and pulled the roots. Nothing. I could do nothing.

Susan Carter

CHAPTER TWELVE

Foster Care

August 1971, North York, Ontario
Susan

We drove north to the suburbs in our social worker's white Toyota Corolla. As we went farther and farther from downtown, the solemnity of our situation became clear to me. I exchanged nervous glances with Marcus. The streetcar and the subway systems did not extend that far out, and without public transportation, we would be stranded wherever Linda left us.

Would we like our foster Mum? Would she like us? My chest tightened in anticipation of her frustration when she discovered we had no clothes except the ones we were wearing.

Half an hour later, Linda parked the car. We followed her through a maze of walkways winding past rows of red brick townhomes with evergreen doors. Finally, she paused and verified the house number on the address card. While we waited for someone to answer the door, I memorized the location of our new home—third door on the left across from the park. Maybe I could make friends on the playground?

I guessed the woman who answered the door to be in her early sixties. Her name was Mrs. Jenkins, and she greeted us with a kind smile that accentuated her wrinkled cheeks. She wore her hair teased into a poof that towered above her forehead, and the telltale residue of hair dye was visible at her hairline.

After a short exchange of pleasantries, Mrs. Jenkins bid Linda goodbye and escorted us into a narrow laundry room smelling of fabric softener. A mid-sized red collie lay in a wicker basket beside the humming furnace. She sat up and wagged her tail.

"This is Lassie." Mrs. Jenkins patted the collie. "This room will be your living space." She motioned with her hand and spoke in a gentle yet firm voice, then tapped the laminated table. "You will eat all your meals, do your homework, and play here." She pointed to the empty bookcase by the back door. "Keep your homework on the top shelf. Store games directly below. You will enter the house through the back door, remove your shoes, and place them on the bottom shelf. Any questions?"

We shook our heads. I could survive where I knew the boundaries. Mrs. Jenkins' organized home was a source of great comfort to me.

The washing machine clicked into its spin cycle, gushing sudsy water from a hose into the cement laundry sink.

Mrs. Jenkins led us through the dining room, crammed with antique furniture, and into the living room. "You may watch TV for half an hour each evening, but only after you have bathed and changed into your pajamas. Now, I will show you to your rooms."

I followed with my siblings as Mrs. Jenkins climbed the carpeted staircase to the landing on the second floor. She paused at the first of two closed doors. "This is the guest room, and the next room is mine. Both of these rooms, as well as the dining room, are off-limits." She locked eyes with me, then the others. "Do you understand?"

I looked at my brother and sister, catching their gazes. The lines of demarcation had been drawn—foster children versus family, each of us in our place.

Three open doors revealed the hall bathroom and the remaining two bedrooms.

"Marcus, this is your room." Mrs. Jenkins pointed to the room farthest from the bathroom. "And girls, the front room is yours."

A print copy of the *Mona Lisa* hung at the top of the stairs; her eyes seemed to follow us as we trailed behind our hostess to enter the front bedroom. Twin beds filled opposite corners. The only decor in the room was a vase of silk flowers, centered on a small vanity that blocked the window.

"I want the bed near the window," Polly said.

Mrs. Jenkins sat on what would be my bed.

"What should we call you?" I pulled back the curtain and looked outside.

"Mum?" Polly offered.

"I'm not your mother." Mrs. Jenkins grimaced. "My kids and grandchildren wouldn't like that."

"Mrs. Jenkins?" I asked.

"No, too formal and sounds awkward in public." Mrs. Jenkins stared at the ceiling, clearly considering.

"What did your other foster kids call you?" Marcus asked.

"Mum Jenkins. It's a balance of cozy and respectful."

We returned her smile. I understood Mum Jenkins' straight-forward manners and reserve, they were part of our Canadian DNA. I had found a friend.

My life—our lives—fell into a comfortable rhythm with Mum Jenkins. I had three nutritious meals a day, a place by the warm dryer to do my homework, and evening walks with the dog. Sometimes she prepared an English dessert then joined us at the laundry room table. My siblings and I sampled trifle, fruitcake, and bread pudding while listening to Mum Jenkins' tales of English traditions and history.

On my tenth birthday, my foster mum prepared an English party. I was so excited, and she even let me invite a girlfriend to join us for the celebration. I would have a *real* party. Mum Jenkins served crackers with cheese, fruit salad, baked chicken with mashed potatoes, a yummy chocolate cake, *and* a birthday cake adorned with pink roses and green leaves on the top, and roses around the base. Two cakes! I was overwhelmed by her generous act of kindness.

After the meal, Mum Jenkins gave me a beautifully wrapped package. I carefully removed the bow and opened the gift. To my delight, the blue leather case contained a complete manicure set with pearly, light blue handles. One by one, Mum Jenkins removed each piece and taught me how to use them.

"I will forever remember this birthday," I said.

"You're double digits now, a young lady," Mum Jenkins said.

I heard it in her voice and saw it sparkle in her eyes, that love I had always craved.

"I've one more surprise for you."

I followed her to the spare room.

She pulled back the down-feathered quilt and patted the satin sheets.

I thought I would burst with gratitude. Only honored

guests spent the night in the spare room, and tonight, I was that person. I threw my arms around Mum Jenkins' neck and whispered in her ear, "Thank you!"

That holiday season, I wanted to give Mum Jenkins a gift for Christmas. Something special to show her how much I loved her.

The stereo softly played Frank Sinatra singing Christmas carols. Mum Jenkins lounged on the sofa, knitting clothes for our Barbie dolls and humming along with her favorite singer. I huddled at the laundry room table with Marcus, scheming ways to raise enough money to buy a present for our foster mum.

I flipped my pen back and forth. "Let's buy perfume."

Marcus shook his head. "No, she already has three unused bottles of rose toilet water on her dresser."

"Well ... she likes candy-coated almonds."

Marcus chewed the eraser on the end of his pencil. "First things first. We need to figure out how to raise the cash before we decide on a gift."

"Sally told me she made twenty dollars caroling last year," I said.

So every evening that December, my siblings and I took Lassie for a walk. In forty-five minutes, we could sing at six households then return home. Christmas week, we filled our pockets with our earnings and headed to the mall. We bought a red stocking with a furry white top and filled it with Mum's favorites: a deck of cards, a compact mirror, red lipstick, Licorice Snaps, and Jordan Almonds.

I heard creaking on the stairs on Christmas morning

and knew Mum Jenkins had gone down to make breakfast. When the aroma of waffles drifted upstairs, my siblings and I slipped into Mum's bedroom and placed the stocking at the foot of her bed. After our meal, Mum returned to her room. I raced to the foot of the stairway and patiently waited, listening, with my brother and sister.

A few moments later, Mum Jenkins leaned over the banister. "Delightful, my dears. What a splendid surprise! Thank you."

I'm sure I saw an extra sparkle in her eyes. Our efforts had been rewarded and the gift well received. Most of all, Mum Jenkins knew we loved her.

CHAPTER THIRTEEN

The Visit

March 1972, North York, Ontario
Susan

A nip of cold lingered in the air on Easter morning, and a light frost coated the ground. I secretly hoped Mum Jenkins would gift each of us a small, cream-filled, chocolate Easter egg. My siblings and I entered the laundry room and found a basket of three huge chocolate rabbits on our table.

"Are these for us?" Polly asked.

Marcus read the label on his rabbit. "Each chocolate weighs an entire pound."

"How do you eat a gigantic candy?" I asked.

"One bite at a time," Mum Jenkins said. "Start with the ear or the foot."

I nibbled at the bunny's ear. Creamy chocolate filled my mouth. "Mmm."

"Now, children, listen closely. Our dinner guests will soon arrive. The Easter treats I bought my grandchildren are the same as yours. One last bite, then I'll hide your candy in the hall closet until my family leaves."

"But why?" Polly asked.

"I can't have them thinking I love you equally, right?"

"Of course not," I mumbled, understanding my place.

"After all, grandchildren are forever," Mum Jenkins added.

"But they'll ask about our candy," Marcus said.

Mum Jenkins grimaced. "I'll hide these until later." She left, then returned and set a basket with nine marshmallow peeps on the top shelf of our bookcase.

I had to wait until her family left to get back my chocolate—we all did. Somehow, it wasn't quite as yummy.

Spring 1972, Toronto, Ontario

I often worried about my brothers we left behind. I hadn't seen David or Thomas in several months. One night I crept into Marcus' room to mention it to him. "If we don't visit them soon, they'll forget us," I said.

"I doubt it. But I'll talk with our foster mum and ask her to arrange a visit." Marcus rolled over and turned off the lamp on the nightstand.

I tiptoed back to my room, carefully avoiding the creaks in the floorboards.

I don't know how it was arranged. But eventually Linda, the social worker, picked us up and drove us to the other side of town. She ushered us to the finished basement of our brothers' foster home and left us alone with them.

Marcus bounced Aulden on his lap. "We're your family," he said.

Aulden's eyes widened. He wiggled, frantically trying to free himself. "No."

Marcus tightened his grip. "Yes, we are." He turned to me for reinforcement. "Tell him, Susan."

How could I explain the complications of our lives to a two-year-old? "They took you away from us when you were a baby," I said. "You're our little brother. Cross my heart."

Tears pooled in Aulden's eyes and spilled over. "Down," he whimpered.

Davie patted Aulden's arm. "He thinks our foster sisters are his real family," he explained to Marcus and me.

Thomas shrugged. "Yea, they told us you're just visiting."

Marcus' expression darkened with anger; I bit my bottom lip. Just visiting? Hadn't their foster parents mentioned we were their *real* family?

That night, Marcus came to my room and sat on my bed.

I dabbed my nose with a Kleenex. "Our baby brother has forgotten us."

"I know, right?" Marcus asked. "I'll tell Linda visiting them once every six months isn't working."

I fell asleep worrying if my youngest brothers would ever again call me *sister*.

A month later, I found Marcus sitting on the laundry room floor and tying his shoes.

"Where are you going? Can I come?" I asked.

"I'm studying for a history exam with my friend, Jeff." Marcus rose and paused in the doorway. "Bye."

A couple of hours later, I stood on Jeff's porch and

knocked on his front door.

Jeff answered. "What are *you* doing here?"

"Looking for my brother."

"He's not here."

"Don't you have to study for a history exam?"

"Took that yesterday."

I walked home forlorn and confused. What was Marcus hiding? And why would he hide it from me?

An hour after I returned home, Marcus entered the laundry room and knelt on the mat to remove his shoes.

"How was your day?" I asked.

"Interesting."

I drummed my fingers on the table. "Hmm. I bet."

"Where's Polly?" Marcus placed his shoes on the shelf by the door.

"Walking the dog."

He studied my expression. "What's wrong with you?"

I stared back at him. Was he kidding? He'd been lying to me, and I didn't know for how long.

Marcus leaned across the table. "I rode the bus and spent the day with Mum," he whispered.

"*What?*" How could he have gone without me? Wouldn't Mum want to see me, too?

"I called Aunt Edith," he said. "She told Mum where to meet me. Jeff's dad gave me a copy of the bus schedule. I cashed in pop bottles and saved up money for the fare."

"Why didn't you take me?"

"Both of us gone for seven hours? Will someone please say *suspicious*?"

"So you were with our Mum all day?"

"Yes." Marcus glared. "You better keep this a secret."

I agreed, just as Polly walked in. Although I

understood the need for secrecy, I was peeved he'd gone to see Mum without me.

Later that night, I sat on the floor in Marcus' room, whispering to him in the dark.

"What did you tell Mum about me?" I asked.

"You received high marks on your transportation project," he said.

That made me happy. Wouldn't Mum be proud?

"And you won't dye your teeth with those bitter red pills before brushing."

I feigned gagging, and we both laughed.

"When can *I* see Mum and Dad?" I asked.

"They're coming to my choir concert next week."

"Does Mum Jenkins know?"

"Seriously? Of course not! And you better not look for them either, because if Mum Jenkins sees you talking together, *they* could get in deep trouble."

My anticipation built as the next Friday approached. On the day of the concert, nothing else mattered to me but seeing Mum and Dad. That evening, Mum Jenkins puttered about the house as if we had nowhere to go and nothing was happening.

"Please, let's go early and get a good seat," I said.

"No worries, dear," she said. "My friend is saving us a spot near the front."

During the program, I struggled to face forward rather than turning around and looking for my parents. Were they nearby? Did they see me? If only I could see them for a few moments.

I fantasized about different scenarios for making contact. If Mum went to the washroom, I could follow her and touch her hand at the sink. We would exchange glances, and she would wink at me. If I passed Dad in the foyer, I'd brush by him and slip a note in his pocket.

When the house lights came on for intermission, I climbed onto my seat backward and knelt, scanning the crowd. Mum Jenkins was preoccupied talking with friends. The auditorium bustled with parents, grandparents, and other guests. They moved much like a hill of ants, so much so I couldn't distinguish one person from another. I wished I knew the color of Mum's coat.

At bedtime, I again crept to Marcus' room. "I searched for Mum and Dad everywhere and never found them." My voice cracked.

"I told Mum Jenkins to sit on the left side, and I told Mum and Dad to sit on the right side. Imagine my shock when you arrived late and sat directly in front of our parents." He sucked in his breath. "I thought I would wet my pants."

I wiped my tears with the bedsheets. "Mum and Dad sat in the row behind us? Why didn't I see them?"

"They hid their faces behind their programs and left before the lights came on for intermission. They couldn't risk getting caught."

If only Mum had made eye contact with me. If only she had given me a smile or winked. Did they see me as a child who was incapable of keeping a secret? How I ached for her touch—couldn't she have brushed past me? That she'd been close enough to touch and hadn't reached out hurt like a burn.

CHAPTER FOURTEEN

Family Bonds

Early summer, 1972, Toronto, Ontario
Susan

Every time Marcus went to Jeff's house, I wondered if he visited Mum. But I never asked for updates. If he could see our mother without me, I wouldn't let him know I cared.

The Agency approved a two-week reprieve for Mum Jenkins. When Mum Jenkins took her vacations, Marcus, Polly, and I stayed with either her daughter, Auntie Theresa, in Toronto, or with her son, Uncle Raymond, in the country. For this trip, Mum Jenkins would be visiting her home in Bristol, England, and we would be staying with Uncle Raymond and his family. Uncle Raymond and his wife, Delphine, cared for their five biological children, three fosters, and occasionally, my two siblings and me.

Auntie Delphine insisted on a weekly ritual she called "family time." For this meal, she prepared a beautiful dinner of roast, potatoes, gravy, vegetables, salad, and dessert. She set the table with fine china and a seasonal centerpiece. But at mealtime, only real family members were allowed at the table. The foster children sat outside and ate relish sandwiches.

After dinner, my siblings and I took turns with Uncle Ray's fosters, washing and drying pots and pans from the family's meal, while listening to their laughter in the adjoining room.

"Are they mean?" I asked Hollie, one of the other foster children.

"They never hit us or yell. I'd say they're generally decent."

"But I've noticed you're the first to be sent to bed and are assigned the dirtiest farmyard chores."

Hollie shrugged. "It's not so bad."

"Anything else I should know about living here?"

"Don't expect a window seat in the car."

I raised my eyebrows. "Got it."

Hollie emptied the drain and wiped down the countertop. "I get it at school, too—the cold shoulder treatment."

My fourth-grade teacher came to mind. I had often sensed her disdain at my inability to read or do figures. I noticed she preferred to invest her time with the quick learners, arranging special projects for them and praising their brilliance.

"I know what you're saying," I said. "My teacher doesn't like me. That's why I don't raise my hand in class."

"You must ask questions. How else will you learn?"

"But I lisp whenever I say the letter s." Heat rose in my cheeks.

"Doesn't your school have a speech teacher?"

"Oh, yes. And I've improved a lot. Listen. Sally sells seashells on the sandy shore. But my classmates still mock me, and my teacher doesn't stop them."

Hollie held out her pinky finger. "Let's promise

always to be kind to one another."

We locked fingers and shook.

When I climbed into my bunk the following evening, I found the bedsheets had been replaced with a plastic mattress cover. I went to the basement, searching for bedding, and found my auntie folding laundry.

I knew Aunt Delphine didn't like me, but I had to ask. "Auntie Delphine? Um, it's just that, well … my bed is unmade."

She slammed down the laundry and brushed back loose strands of hair framing her face.

I studied her fierce appearance, hoping to find a glimmer of sympathy in her steel-gray eyes. Seeing none, I backed away. Clearly, I wasn't one of her priorities.

The following day, I commented to Auntie Delphine about how much the plastic had stuck to me and made me sweat the night before.

She scowled at me. "You can stand to lose a few pounds."

I wondered whose idea it had been to become foster parents—Auntie Delphine's or Uncle Raymond's? Neither of them seemed to enjoy fostering. However, Hollie did say that Uncle Raymond treated her nicely when the other children weren't looking.

"Define nice," I said.

"When I go with him to the feed store, we stop for ice cream on the way home."

Which meant maybe Uncle Raymond was compassionate, after all. Then I overheard him talking with a stranger.

"Are all these children yours?" the stranger asked.

Uncle Raymond chuckled. "Nah, only the cute ones. The others are just fosters."

My throat went dry. God help me, I was one of them—a no-account foster, unvalued, and unworthy of mention.

Mid-summer 1972, Wasaga Beach

Missing my parents didn't lessen with time. I'd seen my younger brothers again—we'd visited with them at a playground near their home. Aulden didn't know us, but that couldn't be changed. I hoped I could rebuild my relationship with them in the future.

Our housing development had many kids, so I always had playmates. Group games like hide-and-seek, chase, baseball, and kick-the-can were the norm.

One morning, Mum Jenkins carried her poached eggs to the laundry room and joined us for breakfast.

"For years, I have spent two weeks of summer vacation with my grandchildren in a cabin at Wasaga Beach," she said. "You could say it's a tradition."

I scooped a fork full of eggs onto my toast. "Where's Wasaga?"

"A few hours north of here on the shore of Lake Huron. Raymond will drive us up there on Friday."

"So, we're coming too?" Marcus asked.

"Oh, yes. The Agency wants you to have a vacation. You might as well tag along with us."

"Are all your grandkids coming?" I asked.

"No, only the oldest three. Brice, Lori, and Kate."

Saturday morning, excitement bubbled inside me. We loaded our suitcases, coolers, and beach supplies into Uncle

Raymond's station wagon. I didn't climb in, but waited, hoping against hope for a window seat. To my surprise, the others piled in the back, and I slipped into the seat by the door. I couldn't believe my good fortune.

"Hop out for a moment, Susan," Uncle Raymond said. "The surfboard goes there."

"But where will I sit?"

"Curl up underneath it."

"Will we all take turns?" I asked.

"Anyone want a turn under the surfboard?" Uncle Raymond asked the others.

Brice tittered, and no one volunteered. Self-pity swamped me. I wished I'd stayed home with Lassie.

Three hours later, we tumbled out of the vehicle. All memory of the discomfort of the journey dissolved when the sun warmed my back, and the cool lake breeze cooled my face. I carried my suitcase up the sandy path to the log cabin nestled on the side of the hill. I had never stayed in a cabin on the lake. That was a treat for rich folks. This would be a glorious adventure.

"Children, you're free to explore the beach," Mum Jenkins said. "Be back for dinner in an hour."

My two-week vacation was extended into three. Each morning I awoke anticipating the adventures that day would bring. We spent countless hours swimming in the lake, hiking in the pine-scented woods, or roasting marshmallows over the campfire.

Uncle Raymond brought the rest of his family up on the weekends, and we joined them in town for wooden rollercoaster rides, cotton candy, and a fifty-cent matinee at the cinema.

I didn't want the vacation to end. Kate and I strolled down the beach on the last day, searching for items to include in a team treasure hunt.

I added a piece of driftwood to our basket. "This is the best summer I've ever had."

"We always have a great time here." Kate knelt in the surf, rinsing sand from shells.

Waves slapped at the shore.

"Your mum scares me," I said. "She's so strict, especially with the fosters."

Kate chuckled. "She is intense at times."

"Do your parents like fostering? It doesn't seem like they do."

"Your feelings are still hurt from being left out of the family dinner."

"There is that. And your parents treat us like we're in the way." I blushed.

"Before my parents began fostering, they promised we would always have special times together. Just us, as a family. Mum says we need those memories. I know it seems mean to you. But one day, you will be gone. And our family will always be together."

"Yes, that's what Mum Jenkins says."

"Grandma didn't have to bring you to the beach, you know." Kate stood and hooked her arm through mine. "She never brought her other fosters."

I picked up a piece of smooth glass and dropped it in our basket.

"We'd best go back and get this treasure hunt started," Kate said.

Arm in arm, we returned to join the others. In that moment, I was content. Mum Jenkins loved me, and Kate was my friend.

After months of waiting and hoping my parents would try to see us, I couldn't wait any longer. I feared if I didn't ask Mum Jenkins to ask for a visit, I'd never see my parents again.

One evening I found her sitting at the antique dining room table, sorting her mail. "May I help you, dear?"

"When can we see our parents?" I asked.

"That's a question for your social worker. I'll call her tomorrow."

The following week, Linda drove us to the Children's Aid Service headquarters. My stomach tossed and turned as we walked down a dimly lit hallway to the receiving room. Many questions swirled in my brain. *Mum and Dad, are you still together? When can we come home?* But since I hadn't talked to them in so long, I didn't want to risk upsetting them. Before reaching the meeting room, I put on my best fake smile.

Mum and Dad stood to greet us as we crowded into the visitation room furnished with six chairs and a small round table.

"Hey, Do-Bee. How's school?" Mum asked.

Hearing Mum use my pet name brought tears to my eyes. I hugged her waist, pressing my face against her warm bosom, breathing in her Lily-scented perfume. "Okay," I said.

"Polly, what do you do with your days?" Dad asked.

"I cut out paper dolls and play with the dog."

"Where are our brothers?" Marcus asked.

"They can't come until this afternoon," Dad said.

Mum sat in one of the chairs then placed her purse on the table. She withdrew three gifts and gave one to each of us.

Mine, a three-piece vanity set, consisted of a matching comb, hairbrush, and mirror. I flipped over the mirror and admired the hand-stitched flower arrangement on the cloth back. "I've never seen a mirror this beautiful," I said.

Mum stroked my long hair. "Remember when I used to fix your pigtails?"

The misery brewing in my soul eclipsed the joy of receiving the gift. I locked eyes with my mother, hoping she'd read my thoughts. *I'd rather have you and my family than a gift.*

The hour passed quickly. What were my parents doing to get us back? Was the agency making things tough on them and hindering our return?

As we prepared to leave, I noticed tears shining in Mum's eyes.

She blew me a kiss. "See you later, alligator."

I pressed the brush set to my heart and followed Marcus into the hallway.

CHAPTER FIFTEEN

Released

Spring 1973, North York, Ontario
Susan

I hadn't seen my parents in many months. I had no idea what was going on with them.

One afternoon, I walked Lassie. We returned home, and I gave a slight tug on her leash, the signal to sit. Saliva dripped from her tongue. I entered the backyard, pulled the gate shut, and reached for the lock.

"Wait up," Marcus called.

Lassie nudged my hand, and I scratched behind her ears.

Marcus leaned over the gate from the outside, pausing to catch his breath. "Mum Jenkins told me the court hearing is next month."

My jaw dropped. I didn't know our parents had given up on us. And why were the proceedings happening so quickly? Soon, we might be available to be adopted by strangers. I had hoped we'd have an extended stay with Mum Jenkins.

"We won't belong to our parents anymore," Marcus

said. "Another family can adopt us."

The sweet scent of a nearby lilac bush seemed to mock my loneliness. Wouldn't Mum and Dad fight for us? Would Children's Aid place us in different homes?

"Most couples only want one or two children," Marcus continued as if he'd read my thoughts. "I bet Children's Services splits us up." He trembled, excitement shining in his eyes as if he were gearing up for the adventure of a lifetime.

My eyes filled with tears.

My brother tried to sound concerned. "Don't worry. We can always ride the subway and meet downtown. If that doesn't work, I promise to write you." He spun on one heel and ran off to share the big news with his pals.

Every ounce of energy drained from my body. I knelt beside Lassie and hugged her neck. With my face buried in her fur, I breathed deeply of her comforting doggy smell. *Must there be more separations? I don't want to lose Marcus and Polly, too.*

Two weeks later

Mr. Clarke, my fourth-grade teacher, tapped his nose. "Susan, are you chewing gum?"

All eyes turned in my direction. He'd caught me. I spat the wet gum into my palm and rolled it into a ball. Several classmates snickered as I placed the sticky wad on the tip of my nose.

Mr. Clarke rapped his pointer on a poster depicting a safari. "There are two distinct types of elephants: the small,

Asian elephant; and the larger, African elephant."

The kid in front of me raised his hand. My teacher recognized him. "Yes, Victor?"

"Why are elephants wrinkled?"

"No one has ever tried to iron them." Mr. Clarke winked.

The entire class erupted in laughter. We all knew that joke.

The recess bell rang. While my classmates filed past, I lingered at my desk, watching Mr. Clarke erase the blackboard.

"Mr. Clarke ..." I swallowed hard, fighting back the tears. I trusted him because I could tell he cared about his students. "The judge might release us soon for adoption."

I knew he was engaged to be married. Wouldn't he and his new wife want kids? Maybe, if I told him I might be available soon, they would pick me.

He turned to me and smiled encouragingly. "But that's good news, right? Now you can be placed in a stable home."

I feigned cheerfulness, but inside I was sobbing. Didn't he see I had given him and his bride the chance to be my parents? Why didn't he understand?

Mr. Clarke resumed his task.

While his back was turned, I wiped my nose on my sleeve and headed for the playground. I should have known that Mr. Clarke's love for his students did not equal parental love. Once again, I had been rejected.

The next day in class, during the reading circle, Mr. Clarke chose to read a book about adoption. Inside, I squirmed as he read about a couple who decided to adopt an orphan. The new parents assured the child of his specialness simply because they had *chosen* him.

Mr. Clarke's voice gently rose and fell like a skiff riding the swells. But in my thoughts a tempest raged.

My parents are worthless, which means I'm worthless. They abandoned me. I'm an unwanted child.

My teacher was sharing all my family secrets with the world. Suddenly, I couldn't sit there in class any longer, listening to him nonchalantly discuss the circumstances of my life, as if my fears and the nightmare I was living were nothing of consequence. My chair clattered to the floor as I sprang from my seat and fled the classroom.

If I no longer belonged to my parents, and no one else chose me, what would become of me? I couldn't bear the thought of further humiliation and rejection.

I entered the washroom and locked myself in a stall, weeping inconsolably. My life resembled an endless roller coaster ride, and I was an unwilling passenger, thrown off balance at every turn. Knots twisted in my gut. Now my worth might rest on being chosen by a random stranger?

Humph. I don't want to be chosen. By Mr. Clarke or anybody. Why couldn't I just stay with Mum Jenkins and have my brothers come live with her, too? At least then I'd have all my siblings with me. And Mum Jenkins to love me. But going away with someone new—my whole body shook with apprehension.

Why had Mum and Dad left us? We were good kids, weren't we? I racked my memory for clues. Would my parents go to the adoption release hearing? Would they fight for us?

A vivid picture flooded my memory. My mother, crying out in agony as she reached back toward the twins, while Dad ushered her to the waiting yellow taxi. Try as I might, I couldn't recall any further effort to reclaim them.

There was also the mystery of my sister, Rose. What

had happened to her?

And now, me and my siblings. There must have been a reason my parents left us. *Think. Think hard.*

I sank to the linoleum floor and pressed my back against the cold cinderblock wall, recalling the night I awoke to find Mum sitting on my bed and sobbing. The winter coat I often slept in slipped down as I reached to take her hand. Light streamed in from the hallway and fell across her face. Fiery resentment smoldered in her eyes, and her expression spoke of bitter hatred.

I shrank back from her. *Was I having a nightmare? Who was the wretched soul sitting on my bed?*

Mum shook a fist of cash in my face. "You'll never know the hell I endured to get this. And for what? Another box of mac and cheese?" She covered her mouth and stifled another sob. The next moment, she left. She hurried down the hall, her footsteps lightly tapping the wooden floor. Then, the back door had clicked shut.

Why hadn't I realized the truth before? Looking back, for the first time, I doubted my parents' ability to care for us. Not that they couldn't if they genuinely wanted to, but at what cost? Now I saw, we children were a terrible burden. However unknowingly, we had driven them to the breaking point, as sure as storm clouds brought rain.

The rhythmic drip from a leaky faucet echoed as I sat there, my world shifting.

When I returned to class, everything seemed to have continued as usual. Mr. Clarke spoke in low tones, assisting a student with his arithmetic. A classmate stood at the wall grinding the pencil sharpener.

But I was a different person. During that hour in the washroom, my childhood ended. My soul aged. I vowed to be more aware of the happenings around me. And from then on, my secrets would stay buried. I would share them with no one, not even teachers who seemed friendly.

June 1973, Downtown Toronto
Madeline

Sitting in the cloth rocker, Madeline tucked her feet up under her and leaned back. Sunlight streamed through an open window, carrying the illusion of a promise that today might be a good day. She rustled the papers in her hands and stared once more at the notice from Children's Services. The court hearing to determine the placement of her children was scheduled for tomorrow.

For the past three years, she had dated around. Hoping to find someone kind who loved her *and* was crazy enough to take her and her children. But she'd found no such man.

Sorrow gripped her. She had no companion, and she was about to lose her children forever. If only she had a good job, she might bring her children to live with her. Children's Aid had offered her training in technical skills. But holding down a job, working nine to five every day? She simply wasn't built for that kind of life. She knew who she was, a high-maintenance, needs-lots-of-TLC kind of gal. Office work would never do for her.

But her babies. Her precious babies …

Still, she knew she'd always lean on others for survival—that's why she needed a man—even when doing so prevented her from providing stability for her children.

Madeline reread the document. "Parents are required

to be present if they have any interest in keeping said children."

I better tell Dave. Despite their animosity, he had a right to know the time to recover their children was coming to an end.

She went to Dave's apartment and knocked on the door.

"What are you doing here, woman?"

"Here's a letter from the Social Services," she said.

"Why do I care what those bureaucrats have to say?"

"It's about the kids. The agency wants to release them for adoption."

Dave grabbed the notice from her. "Over my dead body."

She followed him into the closet-sized kitchen of his efficiency apartment and took a seat.

Dave's face reddened as he laboriously read the letter and its contents became clear to him. "I'm not going to stand for this. I won't allow it!"

Madeline clutched her purse and scooted to the edge of her chair, ready to flee if she felt unsafe.

"No way are *my* boys going to have their last name changed." He shook with suppressed rage. "They can't take away my rights to my kids."

"The custody hearing is tomorrow," she said.

"How long have you known about this?"

"A few days," she said.

"And when were you going to tell me?"

"You know now." Madeline twitched but slightly lifted her chin.

Dave glared at her. "Let me guess. You're not going."

She'd had her chance to be a good mother to them, and she'd failed. At this point, a court appearance was meaningless. "No. The kids will be better off with new parents."

"They're *my* kids, and I'm not giving up on them. I'll go and fight for them. *Alone*."

Anger boiled within her. If Dave had taken care of his family, they wouldn't be having this conversation. Empty words—that's all he'd ever given her. His alcohol addiction still consumed him and controlled how he spent his money. He had no actual means to care for the kids, yet he still pretended he could provide them the best life. Unbelievable.

Dave focused on her. "Now, be gone before I throw you out." He slammed his fist into the wall, shattering the plaster. "You'd better run!"

Madeline fled. She'd done what she came to do.

Ontario Court of Justice
Dave

Dave rode the Metro to the courthouse and sat on a metal bench in the corridor, hoping for an invitation to enter the courtroom. In that moment, he was determined to get back his children. He would not abandon them—he would not be like his father.

As the minutes passed, he shifted. He was worried about his family's future, aching for a drink, and remembering.

Before his parents divorced, his mother had scrimped and saved simply to feed and clothe her seven children. She had shopped at thrift stores. She had re-organized her laundry room and earned money doing wash for others. He still recalled the scent of Clorox that had clung to his mother's hands.

And what had his father done? Wasted money and time at the wharf-side pubs.

Eventually, his mum had saved enough to purchase a General Electric wringer washer. The new-fangled machine had reduced the drying time, allowing her to keep up with the mounds of clothes customers left at her door.

But she still couldn't pay the bills. Desperate for more money, she took a job as a housemaid. Dave hadn't understood his mother's absence or why he and his siblings had to fend for themselves. But now, being a parent, he respected her resolve to care for them.

She'd told him of the night that changed everything. She'd been walking home from work in the bone-chilling wind, shoving her hands into her pockets and grasping the delinquent electric bill. She'd had to search for nighttime work, but even with working double shifts, she wouldn't make enough for their basic expenses, not to mention heating their home.

She'd crossed the road and heard the last strains of a hymn wafting through the open window of a storefront chapel. She went inside and slid into an empty seat on the back row, seeking a simple moment of peace.

The minister behind the pulpit seemed to speak directly to her. "Lay down your burdens and cares at the foot of the Cross. Jesus knows all about you. Today's trial did not take Him by surprise." Then, he spoke of asking God for wisdom and direction. Of falling on God's mercy and asking for forgiveness of sins based on Jesus' death on the Cross.

Right then and there, his mum had bowed her head. *God, help me. Show me what to do.*

She thought of the harsh words she'd yelled at her husband that morning and of her padded timecard. "God, I am a sinner. Please forgive me," she prayed.

And for the first time, she felt clean inside—peaceful enough to laugh aloud, right there in her seat.

Hours later, his mum huddled in their living room, leaning toward the register, a patchwork quilt tucked around her legs. *God, I'm trusting You to help me and breathe new life into my family.* When the clock chimed midnight, she heard his father stumble up the front steps and trip onto the stoop. After kicking the wall to knock snow from his boots, his dad entered, shoulders slumped—a trophy from seventeen years as a shrimp boat captain and hunching over broken nets.

"You look beautiful tonight, love." Dad's words were slurred. "What's different?"

Mum told Dad of asking Jesus to forgive her sins and her plans to take the children to church on Sundays. Dad said that's fine, but he wasn't going.

Then Mum gave Dad an ultimatum. "No more liquor in this house. You need to choose—either the liquor or me."

Dave's dad had moved out the next morning. His parents divorced and his older brothers moved in with their father. His teenage sisters, Dave and his twin brother, Paul, stayed with his mum—after all, they were only eight years old.

Dave admired and praised his mother for her grace and courage during her years as a single mother. But he would never abandon his kids, as his father had done.

He pinched the bridge of his nose. If only he could rewind the last five years, he'd do many things differently. He wouldn't walk away from his kids, he'd find a way to pacify Maddie, and string her along so she'd stay.

I want to be there for my kids. The thought of losing his children, especially his boys, had plagued him all night. His twin, Paul, had died single and childless in an auto accident. His two older brothers had several daughters but no sons. Only Dave had sons who could carry on the family name.

Dave bowed his head. "God, return my kids," he whispered. "Give me another chance, and I promise to be a better man. I promise."

A courtroom assistant approached. "Sir, are you here for the parental rights case?"

"Yes, I—" Dave paused and cleared his throat, trying to hide his slurred speech. "I'm here to defend my right to raise my children."

"One moment, please."

The man went into the courtroom. Dave followed and pressed his ear to the crack between the closed doors, listening.

"The children's father is in the hallway," the assistant told the judge. "He reeks of alcohol."

"I refuse to disgrace this courtroom with drunkenness. We will proceed with the termination of parental rights and release these children for immediate adoption." The judge banged his gavel, ending the hearing.

Dave shuffled out of the courthouse and slumped on the steps. He had failed as a father. He *was* just like his dad.

Soon, he quit his job and made a new life with the homeless.

Susan Carter

CHAPTER SIXTEEN

New Parents

July 1973, Toronto, Ontario
Susan

On a lovely summer day, my siblings and I sat on the swings across from our foster home. Several weeks had passed since the court decided we no longer belonged to our parents. I had no hope of getting to stay with my siblings. After all, who would want six kids?

But Linda's blue eyes had twinkled when she assured us she had that very goal. "I'm doing my best to keep you kids together. I can't make any promises, but I believe in prayer, and I'm asking God for a miracle."

"Like in the angel movies on TV?" Polly asked.

No. Inside, I smirked at my sister. Angels were make-believe like fairies.

Now, I heard the click of Linda's heels on the asphalt sidewalk. She approached, wearing a blue cotton dress that highlighted her baby blue eyes.

"She's beautiful," Polly said.

"Like a princess," I whispered. Gripping the chain of the swing, I muttered to Marcus, "Something tells me she's got a secret."

"I have wonderful news for you children," Linda said. "We've located a couple who are looking for a ready-made family. They are coming to meet you. All of you, including your younger brothers."

My eyes widened, and I dug my heels in the dirt, stopping my swing. The adoption was happening way too fast. I'd just lost my parents forever—

"Are they nuts?" Marcus leaned forward. "They want six kids?"

Linda threw back her head and laughed. "Let me give you the short story. A few years ago, this couple registered to adopt a newborn. But when they called the agency to confirm their position on the waiting list, they were told newborns went to couples in their twenties. This couple was over thirty, but they refused to give up their dream of having children. That's why they called us about meeting you."

"From where?" Marcus demanded.

"How big is their house?" Polly asked.

My heart was hurting so badly. "What's their name?"

"Whoa! One at a time. Wayne Henley is a teacher, and his wife, Bonnie, is a homemaker. She can't wait to take care of you. They just purchased a home with five bedrooms, two bathrooms, and plenty of outside spaces to roam. You'll love it there."

"Where?" Marcus repeated.

"They're from the States."

Marcus jumped off the swing and kicked the dirt.

"Is something wrong?" Linda tried to make eye contact with him.

"I never thought of leaving Canada." He averted his gaze. "Doesn't anyone in Toronto want a kid?"

"Finding a family who'll take older children is a challenge. We listed your names in an international adoption pool. Technically, anyone in the world could adopt you. But America is our neighbor. Right? They speak the same language." Linda leaned against the swing set and shielded her eyes from the sun with her hand. "We're trying to keep you all together."

I cringed inside. *An international adoption pool?* I couldn't believe it. We were at the mercy of anyone crazy enough to adopt a herd.

"Where in America?" I asked.

"A little town in southern Kansas. Mr. Henley grew up in Cheney. He teaches fourth grade at the village school."

Marcus looked up. "In the country?"

"That's correct."

"What's there to do in the middle of nowhere?" he asked.

"You can walk to school, ride bikes, and play with your friends. The Henleys plan is to grow a big garden and plant all kinds of things. You enjoy watermelon, right?" Linda asked Polly and me.

We nodded. But I didn't want to move to the United States simply to get a slice of watermelon. The thought of a country carrot patch with bunnies hopping across the rows was appealing, but the thought of leaving Canada made me feel sick. I wondered as Marcus did, wasn't there any Canadian family who would take us?

Polly's swing squeaked, metal grating on metal, blocking my ability to think. I grabbed her chain and jerked her to a stop.

"Do they have other children?" I asked.

"No, no children. But Mr. Henley's mother lives with them, so you'll get to know her. Everyone is beyond excited to meet you."

I exchanged glances with Marcus. What if we didn't like this couple? What if, after meeting us, they didn't want us?

"You said they're over thirty," Marcus said. "How much over?"

Linda chuckled. "They're in their late thirties. Old enough to be your parents, yet young enough to keep up with all of you."

It sounded too good to be true. There had to be a catch.

"Any pets?" Polly crossed her ankles and began swinging again.

"They have a white and yellow cat named Mush."

"When will we meet them?" Marcus asked, his tone lacking emotion.

Linda's face lit up. "The best part is you don't have long to wait. They're coming next Tuesday."

I knew Mum Jenkins loved us. Why didn't she adopt us? My little body almost couldn't contain my grief. Losing my parents was bad enough, but leaving Canada? If things in Kansas didn't work out, we'd have an awfully long walk back to Toronto.

Child Protective Services Office

I spotted the Henleys as we exited Linda's car. The classy couple, neatly dressed, sat at a shaded picnic table in the park.

I walked behind my brothers, twisting my braided hair. My hopes weren't high, after all, these might be the first set of many prospective parents.

Mr. and Mrs. Henley stood and greeted us with warm handshakes. I could tell from the way they folded their arms across their chests they were aching to hug us. But I wasn't comfortable with that. Even if we ended up with them, would I ever be comfortable in their embrace?

"Darling children." Mr. Henley beamed at each of us. "Bonnie and I are looking forward to having you in our home."

Tears shimmered in Mrs. Henley's eyes.

Davie moved toward the strangers. I grabbed his shirt and pulled him back.

"Susan, a girl your age lives on the next block," Mr. Henley said. "You can walk to school together."

I bit my lip. *If* we became friends …

"The town park is perfect for picnics, and Bonnie can fill a picnic basket with yummy pastries. My, oh my, is she ever a fantastic cook!" He winked at his wife. "I'll have you know she makes the best fried okra in all of Sedgwick County."

We each raised our eyebrows, and quizzical looks passed between us.

"What? You've never eaten okra?" Mr. Henley's eyes crinkled.

We shook our heads.

"Oh, children, you have a real treat coming." His hearty chuckle brought tentative smiles to our faces.

Mrs. Henley sat at the picnic table. Aulden jumped up beside her and scooted close, his face beaming. She placed her arm around his shoulder.

They seemed nice. But I didn't want to leave my friends, my relatives, or my beautiful country. Was there any way other than this adoption to reunite with my brothers?

I was almost twelve, too old to break in new parents. If we moved in with this couple, I'd have to obey their rules, come under their authority. They would discipline my brothers. I didn't know if I'd like that.

And if they were indeed kind like Mum Jenkins, if I let myself call their home mine, if I let myself learn to love them, would I be betraying my birth parents? Just thinking about it all made me nauseous.

The following week I flew with my siblings to Kansas. We spent two weeks with the Henleys in the quiet town of Cheney. On our first day there, they paraded us up and down both sides of the four blocks of Main Street, stopping in every shop, introducing us to the owners and any customers who happened to be present. Our tour also included the public library, where we registered for library cards. The elementary school was closed for the summer, but since Mr. Henley had a key, we were able to see inside.

At the local grocery store, we bought two giant watermelons. We took them home, and Mrs. Henley cut them into fourths and gave each of us a section.

I was stunned. A quarter of a watermelon, all my own. The first bite melted in my mouth and redefined watermelons for me. The fruit was super-sweet, flavor-packed, and crisp. I ate every bit of mine.

At bedtime, Aulden kissed Mr. and Mrs. Henley on the cheek. "Good night, Mother. Good night, Father." Mr. and Mrs. Henley's faces radiated pure joy.

I followed Aulden's example, as did each of my siblings.

Later that evening, Polly and I knelt by our bedroom

window, breathing in the smell of freshly cut grass.

"Are we traitors to call the Henleys our mother and father?" Polly brushed away a tear.

I reached for her hand. "No. It's a title of respect, for now. In time, we'll grow to love them."

"They were so pleased when we said it."

"Yes, they were," I said.

Crickets chirped outside. Train wheels screeched at the grain elevator a block away, skidding to a stop.

"Kansas stars are bright," Polly said. "I've never seen stars twinkle until now."

"That's because we're in the country, and there's no pollution."

"Do you like it here?"

"Hmm," I said. "The townspeople are friendly."

A dog barked in the distance as I pulled back the sheets on Polly's bed. "Come, I'll tuck you in."

We nestled our heads on soft pillows and listened to the lullaby of night sounds. In my mind, I wandered through that Kansas dream house with its spacious rooms, high ceilings, and three staircases. *We could make a home here.*

I marveled at how easily Aulden accepted the Henleys as his parents, but then, he'd never known our birth parents. Not really.

I rolled over and pulled up the sheet. I remembered meeting the friendly townspeople and their welcoming gestures. This could be a fresh start for me and my siblings. This could work.

Summer 1973, Toronto General Hospital

Before we left to go to Kansas, the doctor had discovered a football-sized tumor in Mum Jenkins' abdomen. The agency then moved us to live with Mum Jenkins' daughter, Auntie Theresa, so Mum could concentrate on her health.

When we returned to Toronto, we discovered Mum Jenkins had been hospitalized. Her condition had worsened. Linda told us Mum was dying and drove us to the hospital to say our final goodbyes.

We stood in the sterile cancer ward and spoke in whispers. An ominous cloud of doom permeated the atmosphere and intensified the sadness etching Mum's face and lacing her voice. For the entire twenty-minute visit, her eyes glistened with unshed tears. No one dared to verbalize the obvious—the death angel hovered nearby.

At the close of our visit, Mum Jenkins walked with us to the elevator. "Goodbye, children. I love you."

"I love you, too." Marcus gave her a gentle hug. He turned and glared at me with a look that said *Say something. Speak up.*

But I couldn't. I pressed my spine against the back wall of the elevator. I dared not speak. If I'd done so, I would have completely fallen apart. But inside, I screamed, *I love you! You are the world's best Mum, and I will never forget you. Never.*

I wanted so badly to run to her side, throw my arms around her waist, and hold on tightly. As if my doing so would keep her from leaving this world. But I couldn't say goodbye. I simply couldn't.

I'll return someday and bring you flowers, Mum. Yes, that's what I'll do. You wait and see.

As the elevator door slid shut, I blew her a kiss.

CHAPTER SEVENTEEN

Roadblock

August 1973
Susan

Around me, Toronto International Airport bustled with
passengers lugging their suitcases to various destinations.
Finally, my siblings and I were going to live together. There
would be no more separations, and no more foster care, only
a future full of rainbows and happiness. Our happily ever
after would begin with a flight to our new home.

Linda shooed all of us down the jetway and onto the
plane. We were headed to the heartland of America, the land
of Oz. I worried about living in the middle of nowhere.
Already, I longed for the mobility and independence that
came from living near the metro. How far could I travel on a
bicycle? Was there anywhere to go? How strange it would
be to live in a quiet little town, void of the hustle and bustle
of city life.

At the sight of the aircraft, my brothers jumped up
and down with excitement. The pilot greeted them with a
golden pair of American Airlines wings and helped pin the
emblems to their shirts. My brothers' eyes shone with

anticipation of an adventure.

The six of us filled an entire row. We chattered about our future, our voices joining the low hum filtering through the cabin.

The pilot's voice blared from the speakers. "We have permission to queue on the runway. This flight goes from Toronto to Wichita, Kansas."

I glanced out the window and brushed a tear. *O Canada, glorious and free. My country, my home. Must I leave?* A lump formed in my throat.

The jet engines came to life, vibrating my seat. Thomas pressed his face to the window as the plane pulled away from the terminal. I breathed in the stale air and readjusted the overhead vent.

Then without warning, the aircraft slowed, stopped, and pulled back to the gate. The cabin door popped open, and two officials wearing navy uniforms and security badges boarded the plane. Passing through the first-class section, they made their way to economy seating.

"Cool," Davie whispered. "I bet they're after some criminal."

Passengers eyed their neighbors with suspicion. Except for the whoosh of air vents, the cabin grew quiet. We peered over seats to catch a better view of the happenings as the officers continued to the back of the plane, scrutinizing every passenger, then turned and made their way back up the aisle.

I slipped down into my seat and re-clicked my seatbelt. Behind me, one of the officers spoke with Linda.

"Are these children with you?"

"Yes. I am their social worker."

"Retrieve your belongings and come with us. And bring the children with you, of course."

I felt the stares of other passengers as the officers escorted us back to the tarmac. I lowered my gaze, humiliated. Surely, they didn't think Linda was kidnapping us?

Aulden wailed. "I want to ride the plane."

"Hush!" I said. "We'll catch the next flight."

Back in the terminal with our backpacks in tow, we followed the officers to the ticket counter and watched wide-eyed as they escorted Linda into an interrogation room.

An associate rolled her eyes and slammed her notebook. "Great. Now I'm a babysitter." She led us to the staff lunchroom. After instructing Marcus to purchase snacks from the vending machine, she left.

I sought an isolated corner and collapsed onto a folding metal chair. As if in a nightmare, I watched my siblings but remained emotionally detached. Davie and Thomas chased each other around chairs and under tables, unchecked. Polly pulled a strand of hair from behind her ear and stuck it into her mouth. Marcus dropped the coins he'd been given to purchase snacks in his pocket and sat, pensive and holding a whimpering Aulden.

Could Children's Services have gotten it wrong? Were we their first international adoption? The notion was hard to believe. Maybe this was our chance to stay in Canada?

Either an hour or an eternity later—I don't know which—Linda returned with a sheepish grin. "Kids, I am so sorry for this terrible mix up. Unfortunately, we don't have the proper documents to move you to Kansas."

"We're not going?" I gripped Polly's hand and squeezed it repeatedly.

Linda nervously clutched her handbag, digging around until she pulled out her lipstick and applied it with a trembling hand. "Oh, yes. Goodness. You're still going."

"When will we fly to Kansas?" I asked. "Tomorrow?"

"Well … I can't say for certain how long it will take to process all the necessary paperwork. But I can say we'll do our best to move things along quickly."

"What about Mother and Father?" Aulden smeared tears across his face.

Aulden's sensitivity and concern for others startled me. I realized that in his heart, he was already adopted.

"They'll be waiting for us at the airport," Aulden continued. "Mother promised we could stop at the place where the trains deliver the hamburgers."

Linda knelt, pulled a handkerchief from her purse, and dried Aulden's tears. "I called your mom and dad," she said. "I'm positive your mother will keep her promise. It will just happen on another day." She hugged him gently. "Are you okay?"

Aulden sniffed and shrugged.

"Where will we sleep tonight?" Marcus asked.

"We have spoken with your foster families, and they are waiting for you," Linda said.

I looked at Marcus. This meant David, Thomas, and Aulden were going one way; Marcus, Polly, and I would be with Auntie Theresa.

"On the bright side, we'll start with the photographer. You'll each receive your own passport. Isn't that exciting?"

"What about lunch?" Thomas asked.

"Right," Linda said. "Let's do lunch."

My stomach dropped. Returning to Auntie Theresa's was a problem. Rather, her son Parker was a problem. I stole a glance at Marcus and caught him biting his nails. This could not be good.

Linda parked in front of Auntie Theresa's and held the door open as we piled onto the sidewalk.

Auntie met us at the door. "Where's your luggage?"

"Their bags will be delivered tomorrow morning." Linda kept her voice cheerful.

"Should I enroll them in school?"

"Hold off for a few days."

Auntie grimaced. "Children, go along inside while I speak with Miss Linda."

I felt sorry for Auntie Theresa. I'd walked past the basement window many times, pretending not to hear her husband cussing her out or complaining of her incompetence as a housekeeper. She spent many hours a day in that dingy basement feeding clothes through the rollers of an antique washer, mingling her tears with the wet laundry. Upstairs, piles of dirty dishes awaited her. The few times she ventured outside, she usually ended up refereeing fights between her four rowdy children and the fosters—us.

What made matters worse, Auntie's oldest son, Parker, delighted in tormenting Marcus. It seemed anytime Parker did something wrong, Marcus got the blame and the punishment.

From our first week with Auntie Theresa at the end of June, we had asked her permission to spend the day at the public pool every Saturday. At least, that's where we told her we were going. She seemed relieved, and she didn't have the time or energy to wonder about our absence at lunch or verify our whereabouts.

In reality, Marcus had called our birth mum and arranged for her to pick us up near the park. For the rest of the summer, we spent our Saturdays cruising around

Toronto with our mother in her boyfriend's convertible. The wind swept back my hair and blew away any attempt at conversation. I wished we could spend time with Dad, too, but he didn't know about our outings.

Seated in the back of that fancy car, I mulled over the fact that Mum had already released us for adoption. I watched her, memorizing her every expression and mannerism. I loved her unconditionally but built a wall around my emotions and prepared to let her go.

We were still in limbo—waiting to see what would happen with the international adoption yet sneaking off to see Mum on Saturdays.

One evening, I sat with Marcus on the braided rug in his attic bedroom, reviewing the events of the day.

"I hate it here," Marcus said. "Parker sets the traps and screeches like a hyena when I get the blame."

"You pester him," I said.

Marcus cocked his head. "Whose side are you on?"

Earlier that afternoon, Parker had soaked us with the water hose. When Marcus retaliated, Auntie sent him to bed early and without supper.

"Here's the plan," Marcus said. "Go downstairs and head for the kitchen. Pretend you're getting a drink. When no one's watching, we'll run out the back door, sprint across the yard, climb the fence, and hide in the woods until the coast is clear."

I propped my elbow on my knee and cupped my chin in my hand. "Your clothes will catch on the fence."

"Nope. I've been practicing for days. I cleared it in

thirty-seven seconds flat."

Across the hall, Auntie's daughter snored like a hibernating bear.

"It's her asthma," I said, buttoning my sweater.

"Mum and Dad need us," Marcus said. "If we go back home, they'll stop running to the bars and take care of us. But first, they need us to come back. Right?"

I shrugged but couldn't say I remembered them ever truly taking care of us.

"Listen," Marcus said. "When Auntie sent me inside earlier, I phoned Mum. She'll meet us at the park at nine o'clock sharp tonight. Coming?"

Again, a tremendous snore interrupted our conversation. I leaned against the side of my brother's bed. Marcus rose and headed for the hall. The loose steps squeaked as he descended.

Ten minutes later, I, too, went to the kitchen for a glass of water. But Marcus had disappeared. I ran outside, letting the storm door slam behind me as I frantically called his name. "Marcus, wait for me!"

We were scheduled to leave for America the following week. This was our absolute last chance to reunite with our parents, and I missed it. I should have trusted Marcus and followed his plan. Why had I hesitated?

The fact that Marcus had run away caused an uproar throughout Children's Services.

A couple of evenings later, Linda showed up at Auntie Theresa's. "Hop in the car, girls," she said. "Let's take a ride."

I hadn't seen or heard from Marcus since he left. I hoped he was alright.

As we zoomed down the highway, Linda gripped the steering wheel. "We're going to a meeting to discuss your adoption." An icy tone laced her words.

Polly studied my face, but I merely raised my eyebrows. An after-hours appointment with Linda? Were we in trouble? I'd never seen Linda this upset or angry.

The empty hallways at the Agency seemed charged with an eerie quiet. Then, through the smoked glass window of a conference room, I recognized three forms—Mum, Dad, and Marcus.

What?

I entered the room with Polly and Linda. My sister and I took the seats opposite our family.

Linda moved to the head of the table, pressed her lips together, and gripped the back of the chair. Everyone sat perfectly still, waiting for her direction. The hum of the fluorescent lights filled the silence.

Were we there to discuss the adoption with our birth parents?

"The majority of the children we place for adoption are under five years of age. As older children, you have clear memories of your birth parents," Linda said.

We all knew that.

Linda cleared her throat. "You love them."

Yes … and?

Linda grimaced. "Memories of your biological parents could make it hard for you to love your adopted parents. In adult terms, we would call that a division of loyalties, which could create conflict and prove to be the foundation for problems in an adoptive situation."

I squirmed. I didn't understand what Linda was

saying. Was she trying to confuse us? Something had to be wrong. It sounded like she was canceling our adoption.

Linda waved her hand in my parents' direction but kept her gaze on Polly and me. "Your parents have assured us they are back together and that their living situation is stable. They want to keep you."

Our parents love us. A warmth, like heated oil washed through me, soothing my shattered self-image. My parents were fighting to get us back. I wanted to go with them, right?

For the first time since we entered the room, Linda made eye contact with Dad and Mum. "You're free to leave. All of you, together. Right here and right now."

Polly and I remained glued to our chairs.

I was speechless. All summer as we secretly cruised Toronto, I had dreamed of this moment. I imagined our family reunited with Dad, driving us on a Sunday afternoon road trip just like the old days when we lived in Dartmouth. To see them pretend, even for a moment, that things could work out between them warmed my heart. But I also knew a fresh start with Mum and Dad was only a fantasy.

Dad's chair scraped loudly against the floor as he scooted away from the conference table, as if to take Linda up on her offer and leave with all of us in tow.

Linda raised a hand. "Sir, just a moment, please." She turned to Polly and me. "Follow me."

We walked with her to an adjoining office, and she closed the door.

"Neither of you has uttered a word." Linda's tone resonated with kindness yet reflected the seriousness of the situation. "And I can't read your minds. Can you share with me what you're thinking?"

Polly stared at the floor, smacking on her thumb. Her

go-to comfort mechanism, even at nine years old.

I pinched my neck. The pain I'd seen shining in my parents' eyes, the fear of losing us forever—I could ease that pain by going home with them. But wait. Did they have a home?

And what about my younger brothers? If I left there with Mum and Dad and Marcus and Polly, would the agency send them *alone* to Kansas to live with strangers? Would I lose them again when I was so close to getting them back? How could this be happening?

Hadn't the whole agency of social workers done their homework, evaluated our parents as caregivers, and found them lacking? Were Linda and Children's Services copping out by asking us to decide for ourselves?

"Susan, look at me." Linda sat beside me and took my hand. "How do you feel about going home with your parents?"

I lifted my head to meet her gaze. "I've seen my parents fight a million times! The patch-up between them is a lie. They're faking it to fool you into sending us back."

Should I tell her about the secret summer drives? Despair overwhelmed me. I couldn't verbalize my emotions or explain all my siblings and I had gone through.

Summoning my last ounce of courage, I plunged on. "Are you sending us back? If you do, next week we'll be on the streets again scrounging for ..." My voice broke. "My parents can fend for themselves."

Linda's eyes widened, and I could see she understood.

"We have no future in the ghettos." I hugged my sister. "I want to go with my brothers to America. And Polly is coming with me." The strength and resolve in my voice shocked me.

"A child your age shouldn't have to analyze these things," Linda whispered. "This afternoon, my boss insisted we reunite you with your birth parents, and I begged him to reconsider. I have fasted and prayed all day for God to intervene and open a way for you to continue with your adoption." She brushed away a tear and squeezed my hand. "Now, at your request, we will send you to Kansas."

I almost crumpled to the floor with relief. I was glad I'd spoken up, because she'd listened and acted quickly, but I knew this was it. My family would never be reunited, ever.

Linda stood. "I'll inform your parents and Marcus of your decision."

Polly laid her head on my shoulder, groaning. We huddled together, waiting for Linda's return. I cried so much, my tears ran down my cheeks and dripped onto Polly's hair.

Linda escorted us to an exit route for staff. "Let's go this way and avoid an awkward encounter with your family. You've had enough drama for one evening."

As I trudged behind Linda, skirting the scaffolding and remodeling debris lining the hallway, a crushing burden of guilt intensified within me. Had I just rejected my parents? I longed for one last loving glance, one last hug. If only I could run into their arms and weep.

Mum and Dad. Don't be mad at me for going to America. It's just that I'm struggling to survive. Please understand. I'll always love you.

As we rounded the corner of the final corridor, we ran smack-dab into my parents, exiting from the public access hallway.

Linda held out her hand, signaling for us to wait. Mum, Dad, and Marcus lowered their heads and pushed past us to the exit. Marcus locked eyes with mine; his look held a blend of anger and disappointment. I understood how hard he had worked to reunite our family. Yet, I betrayed him by choosing to go to America.

Awash with shame, I lowered my gaze.

We crossed the parking lot, ignoring my parents and Marcus waiting at the bus stop. At the car, Polly hesitated, turning to watch our family board the streetcar.

No, you don't, sister. I grabbed Polly's hand and pulled her into the car. By the time we buckled up, Polly had resumed her vigorous thumb-sucking.

On the way back to Auntie's, Linda offered to stop for ice cream. I watched as Polly licked her cone, but I had no appetite.

I couldn't imagine the pain I had just caused my parents. My only hope was tomorrow would be a new day. Maybe a day full of sunshine.

CHAPTER EIGHTEEN

Welcome Home

September 1973, Cheney, Kansas
Susan

Twelve hundred miles separated the concrete jungle of downtown Toronto from south-central Kansas. In anticipation of the heat, the day we flew to our new home my sister and I braided our long hair and donned cool, cotton dresses.

After we arrived, I discovered some distinct cultural differences. When I reported on a hockey game for a speech assignment, my teacher docked me for irrelevant information, and no one in my sixth-grade class ever ate rhubarb pie.

On the upside, surprisingly, I won a contest for perfectly reciting the inscription on the Statue of Liberty. And I learned Kansas was known as The Sunflower State.

Father had told his students that he and his wife were adopting six siblings from Canada. They went home and told their parents, who told their neighbors. In no time, the whole town had learned of us.

We soon realized the town of Cheney knew no

strangers. Everyone seemed to be at least friends, and more likely, relatives. Everybody's cousin or second cousin twice removed lived just around the corner. Like a web, those relationships connected every family and wove through multiple generations. And this tight-knit community extended a warm welcome to my siblings and me.

The city council threw us a welcome party. They called it "Christmas in September." The entire community eagerly participated. Neighbors brought gifts of bedding, towels, toys, and bicycles. They filled the pantry and overflowed the freezer. One farmer donated a year's supply of milk, which meant we drank three gallons of milk a day and had extra cream for churning butter and making homemade ice cream.

Our first month in Cheney, Mother made sandwiches to order, just the way we liked them. She wrote our names on tiny pieces of paper and used toothpicks to mark each one. Every time I smelled chocolate chip cookies baking in the oven, I ran to the kitchen and licked the mixing spoon. Mother permitted us to eat cookies anytime we wanted, even in the middle of the night. So, I did.

Then our honeymoon ended when Mother set a tray of unmarked sandwiches in the center of the table. "These are all the same. They contain two slices of cheese, mayonnaise, and a lettuce leaf. If you're hungry, eat. If not, I'll see you at dinner." She made eye contact with each one of us. "And no more dipping into the cookie jar without permission."

Apparently, the time had come for our little family to settle into a new norm.

October 1973

Since being reunited with my siblings, I brooded over them like a mother hen, striving to ease the transition into our new home.

On one occasion, four-year-old Aulden and I played on the swing set in the backyard.

"What do you do while we're at school?" I asked.

"Play with the cat and take naps."

The back screen door squeaked, and Mother stuck her head out. "Aulden, come here, please."

My brother pumped his legs harder and swung higher.

"Hey. Didn't you hear Mother calling you?" I grabbed his swing. "You'd better go."

The intensity of his gaze bore into my soul. "Who is my mother? The lady in the doorway?"

I blinked.

"She's mum number four," he said, jumping off the swing.

Although Aulden seemed resilient, he had been deeply hurt. I cringed inside as I thought back to the painful start of his life.

November 1973

Trips with a large family presented unique challenges. Every Saturday, we piled in the white Suburban and drove an hour to K-mart in Wichita. Once in the department store, we wandered the aisles while our parents completed their shopping. An hour later, my family gathered at the registers and loaded into the car for the trip home.

On one such Saturday, we settled into the car with the day's purchases. Father turned over the engine and clicked the car in reverse.

Aulden whimpered.

"What's the matter?" Father looked over his shoulder, guiding the Suburban out of the parking space.

Aulden's eyes widened with distress.

"He probably has a tummy ache," Mother said. "He'll be alright."

Father drove across the parking lot and paused at a yellow light.

Aulden wailed.

"What on earth!" Dad pulled into traffic, made an immediate exit at the first turn-off, and came to a stop.

Sobs shook my brother's body.

Mother climbed into the back seat and gently lifted four-year-old Aulden onto her lap. "There now, honey. What's wrong?"

After a few moments, Aulden paused for a breath. "I don't want to leave Davie behind."

"We're not leaving anyone," Mother said.

Father counted heads. "Well, for crying out loud." He cranked the steering wheel and did a U-turn, retracing our steps to K-mart.

The sight of Davie standing outside the department store brought sunshine to Aulden's face.

Davie climbed into the car, grinning. "I knew you'd come back. How far did you get before you missed me?"

Had Aulden's babyhood wounds heightened his sense of compassion and keen awareness of the needs of others? After all my siblings and I had been through, I vowed to be a part of their lives, forever.

February 1974

"Susan, I'm not convinced," my drama teacher said during class.

Sigh. I would have to dig deeper if I wanted to get it right.

Closing my eyes, I visualized myself outside the liquor store, watching through the window as Dad had pulled out his wallet and handed the cashier his paycheck. An icy wind had penetrated my jacket. Shivering, I held open the door as Dad exited the store while winking at me, his arms loaded with cases of whiskey. My cheeks had flushed with embarrassment for us both. Anger at his choices had shot through my veins.

Now, I stood before my classmates and glared at them. "I *hate* washing dishes."

A student on the front row shuddered. "Grief. It's just a household chore."

"Yeah," said another, "I saw the fire in your eyes and heard the hatred in your voice. How do you do that?"

"Now that's what I'm talking about," my teacher said.

My stomach quivered as I returned to my desk. That was a close call. I had given my classmates a glimpse into my soul, my guarded history.

After class, I lingered in the bathroom, studying my face in the mirror. My classmates were right. The smoldering storm of bitterness darkening my eyes made me resemble a hardened criminal.

I shivered. *Who am I? A twelve-year-old with a load of emotional baggage?* I washed my hands and grabbed a paper towel. *Yes, I carry the burden of a dark past. If only I knew how to move on.*

At home that evening, my family gathered in the living room. Father sat in the wooden captain's chair with his Bible open on the tablet armrest reading from the Gospel of John. He shared stories of how Jesus touched people and transformed the broken and the hopeless.

I reflected on my birth parents and the drama that accompanied their lives. Would I grow up to be just like them? Could Jesus reach beyond my past and rescue me from brokenness, from a life of misery, from a road bound for disaster?

"Children, pay attention," Father said. "Continuing at John 1:12, 'But as many as received Him, to them He gave the right to become children of God, to those who believe in His name:'"

With every fiber of my being, I wanted to be a daughter of God. Did that verse mean *anybody*? Even a nobody, like me? My soul cried out for hope, joy, and purpose. Spending eternity with God? That would be a bonus.

A few days later, I found my father in the recording studio on the second floor of our home. I stood in the hallway and waited as he adjusted the volume knobs and spoke into the microphone. "This concludes another broadcast of *Glorious Freedom*. Thanks for joining us, folks. And be sure to tune in next week for more thrilling teachings from God's Word."

Father removed the headset and glanced in my

direction. "How can I help you, dear?"

"I believe Jesus died to make me a child of God."

"And are you ready to accept Him as your Savior?"

"Yes."

"Fantastic. Wait here while I call for your mother."
Father sprang from his chair and kissed me on the cheek.

Mother came, sat beside me, and took my hand.
"Now, dear, when you pray, ask Jesus to forgive your sins
and invite him into your heart."

I bowed my head and closed my eyes. "Jesus, thank
You for dying on the cross to pay for my sins. Please come
into my heart and teach me to be a Christian. Amen."

In an instant, a weight of darkness and smothering
anger released from my soul. And a sense of newness
rushed in, flooding my being with radiant hope.

I threw my arms around my mother's neck and kissed
her cheek. "Twice adopted," I said.

Father threw back his head and laughed for joy.

On my way back to my room, I glimpsed my profile
as I passed the mirror in the hall, then backed up for a
second look. To my amazement, the reflection showed a
smiling young girl. My face radiated peace, and the look of
my eyes had softened. They sparkled with happiness.

Unbelievable.

Years of anger and anxiety had melted from my
countenance. A sense of wholeness washed over my spirit,
flooding my soul with hope.

Through Christ, I had become a new person. Through
Christ, I would start a new life full of purpose and potential.

Joyful tears spilled down my cheeks.

I would chart a new destiny with the Holy Spirit as
my guide.

March 1974

One by one, each of my siblings had a private meeting with our parents. I didn't understand the secrecy.

When my turn came, I walked up the back staircase and entered the office. Mother sat in the cushioned captain's chair, and Father reclined in the swivel office chair at his desk. I sat on the leather tripod stool by the door.

"We have been working with a team of lawyers to complete the paperwork for your adoption. You are ours, dear," Father said. "There are only a few more questions to answer, and the government will have all your information. Your birth certificates will be re-written to show our names as your parents." He paused. "This is your chance to change your name."

What was Father saying? I expected only my last name would change with the adoption.

"We understand why you may want to keep your first name," Father continued. "It's familiar to you, part of your identity. But a middle name is primarily used on formal documents. Your siblings have all changed their middle names."

I hadn't thought of changing my first or middle name.

Mother and Father exchanged loving smiles. "Now, if your mother and I had birthed a little girl, we would have named her Rebekah Susannah."

Mother leaned forward. "I've always loved the name Rebekah."

"Your first name will be Rebekah, but we can call you by your middle name, Susannah, which is a variation of

Susan. It will sound familiar." Father seemed to feel that settled the matter.

Mother watched me intently. "Or … we could switch the names and call you Susannah Rebekah."

I blinked, trying to wrap my mind around the implications of a name change. Father and mother were serious. *Hmmm.* I had never cared for my middle name. One-syllable "Lynn" lacked flare, but a two-syllable middle name intrigued me.

"Okay," I said.

Relief washed over Mother's face.

"I like the name Sarah," I said, thinking of Grandma Nan.

"What?" Father slapped his thigh and rocked back in his chair. He shot a surprised look at mother. "Where on earth did that come from?"

Mother's blue eyes pooled.

"The initials S. S. H. sound like a battleship." Father sucked in a deep breath, then his tone softened. "S. S. H. is an awkward combination of initials, at the very least."

As the tension deepened, anxiety clouded my thoughts. I stared at the wall, fighting back the tears.

Mother's soft hand caressed mine. "Why *Sarah*?"

"My grandmother's name is Sarah."

The love pouring from Mother's eyes gave me courage. I swallowed the lump in my throat. "By taking it as my own, I'll always have a part of her with me."

Mother patted my hand. "Well, now, let's see if those two names are compatible."

"Great idea." Father reached for the *Name Your Baby* book. "Let's see … Susan, Susanne, and Susannah all come from the same Hebrew word meaning 'lily.'" His demeanor switched to teacher mode. "The lily is a unique flower. The petals repel dirt particles and ensure the flower remains clean, which is why the lily symbolizes purity."

"Beautiful," Mother said.

"I love Lily of the Valley perfume," I said.

Father cleared his throat. "Yes, well, let's move on. Sara, Sarai, and Sarah are also of Hebrew origin, and the translation is 'princess.' Bottom line, the full, literal meaning of your name would be 'lily princess' with the spiritual significance of 'princess of purity.'"

A sense of peace replaced the tension. Father's arms relaxed, the baby book fell into his lap.

"Quite a name to live up to," Mother smiled.

I had a new name, Susan Sarah, and a new identity, *purity princess*. I was thrilled.

CHAPTER NINETEEN

Growing Pains

May 1974, Cheney, Kansas
Susan

We were all sitting at dinner when Thomas passed a cup to Polly, accidentally bumping his own glass and spilling milk all over the table.

Father huffed. "Can't we sit down for one meal without you kids causing a mess?" He reached for the bread and knocked the jar of pickles into his lap. Juice soaked his pants and dripped onto the floor.

I hid behind my napkin, suppressing snickers.

Father left the table, returning moments later with clean pants. Once seated, he reached for Mother's hand. "Children, tomorrow is Mother's Day, and we have special guests coming for dinner."

"Who?" we chorused.

"Our social worker, Evelyn Middlestat, and a little girl named Valorie."

"How old is she?" Polly asked.

"Eight."

"Yay," Polly said. "She's a year younger than me."

"Is she Mrs. Middlestat's daughter?" I asked.

Father and mother exchanged glances. "No, Valorie needs a home. Your mother and I have prayed about this, and we want to adopt her."

Mother beamed with joy and kissed Father on the lips. "The perfect Mother's Day gift."

But we just got here. We were still getting used to being a family. I wasn't ready to share my new parents. I tapped my foot under the table. How could I open my heart to a new sister when at times mine still ached and bled?

The next day as Evelyn's car pulled into the driveway, we all peeked through slits in the blinds. A blonde-haired girl sprang from the back seat and sprinted onto the front porch. Mother waited for the doorbell to ring, then answered.

"Good morning, Valorie," Mother said. "Welcome home."

Valorie's green eyes gave us the once-over then focused on Mother. "Where's the cat?"

I studied Valorie and saw that we were as different as salt and sugar. Valorie seemed to be at ease with herself. She spoke her mind, straightforward and unreserved.

On the other hand, I was self-conscious of my body and thought out each word before speaking. Although we shared similar histories of being abandoned by our parents, and I empathized with her plight, I struggled to welcome her with open arms.

My life took on a new dimension with Valorie in the mix. Her boisterous manners grated on my nerves. Yet despite the personality clashes, I sensed her desire to connect with our family.

A month after her arrival, I sought solace in my room, working on a sewing project. The thread broke, so I released the presser foot and withdrew the material.

Valorie entered the bedroom and stood beside me. "I have a new middle name," she said.

"Nice."

"Are you going to guess?"

I rolled my eyes. "Anne."

"Nope."

"Kim."

"One more guess," Valorie said.

"I'm busy. Just tell me."

"Jean."

"But that's Polly's name."

Valorie bit her lip. "And Mother's."

"Polly had it first. Pick your own name."

"Mother said we can share."

I gave Valorie a long stare. Rethreading the sewing machine, I bent over my work and ignored her. *Must she copy everything we do?*

The tension between Valorie and me increased. I simply couldn't cope with her aggressive personality and opinionated nature.

After spending the weekend with a girlfriend from church, I returned home to find Valorie as my new roommate, whereas when I left, she had been Polly's. Weary, I climbed into bed and pulled the blanket over my shoulders.

Scratch, scratch. I had no idea what the sound was. I only knew it came from the bathroom.

I rolled over, pulling the pillow over my head.

"Squawk!"

I sprang from the bed and rushed to the bathroom.

"Bawk. Bawk. Bawk!" A red hen slid down the side of the tub.

I spun to face my sister with my hands planted on my hips. "A chicken?" *Really?*

"Mother said I could keep her in here. She's not safe outside."

"Believe me, she's not safe here." I pursed my lips and marched straight to mother.

"It's just a chicken," Mother said.

"But the clucking keeps me awake. And chickens have lice. And what about the mess in the bathtub? It's not sanitary."

"Humor her."

I rolled my eyes. *Right. Like you'd say yes if I asked for a zebra.*

"Just wait. Next week she'll bring home a ferret," I called over my shoulder.

Unfortunately, I was right.

I wasn't allowed to spend too much time alone in my room.

"It's not healthy," Mother said.

On rainy days, I curled up on the love seat in the playroom, reading a book, and watching my brothers build cities out of wooden blocks. Their patience amazed me. They spent hours building intricate structures and complex bridges connecting a maze of roads and tunnels.

That particular morning, my brothers exchanged high-fives, divided their Hot Wheels, and settled in to enjoy their wooden block creation.

I set down my book and walked over to their town. "We live in Kansas. Storms and tornadoes happen here all the time." *Time for a life lesson.* "Here comes a tornado." I shuffled and spun through their town, knocking down blocks.

"Nooo!" they shrieked.

Their cries pierced my conscience. What had I done?

I fled to my bedroom closet and wept bitterly. Did meanness lurk in a dark chasm of my soul? *God, forgive me. Would You please take every hint of malice from my life?*

The following day, once again, I sat in the love seat, reading a book, watching my brothers rebuild their block city.

Valorie entered the room as the boys sorted their toy cars. "Here comes a tornado," she said.

"Nooo!" my brothers sobbed. Buildings and bridges crashed in every direction.

A moment later, Mother stomped into the room and shook a finger at me. "Young lady, go to your room this instant."

"But I—" I glanced at Valorie, but she'd turned to pick up the cat, leaving me to take the blame.

"No backtalk. Go." Mother pointed to the door.

I hurried to my bedroom closet and sank to the floor. When the hallway steps creaked, I scrambled out of the closet and dove under my bed.

Valorie knew about my secret place in the closet and checked there first. I smiled at my genius in outsmarting her. Then she paused at the dresser and knelt.

Shoot. How did she find me?

"I'm sorry," Valorie said.

Tears stung my eyes.

"Look, I know you're under there. Your shoes are

sticking out," she said.

I grimaced and drew in my telltale feet.

"Can we be friends?" Valorie asked.

"I'm trying."

"It's hard for me, too. You all are blood brothers and sisters. I don't even look like you."

I swallowed a lump in my throat. True. That must be difficult.

"Friends?" Valorie asked.

"Friends."

I wanted to embrace her as a sister, but I couldn't take that step. Friends? Yes, that was a good starting place.

June 1974

I found Mother sitting in the dining room at the walnut table with pieces of wood and carving tools arranged in front of her. "The annual county fair is the second week of August. All the 4-H children display the things they've worked on. The entries are judged, and prizes are given."

"Like what kinds of things?" Davie asked.

"Since this is farm country, many will bring animals for the livestock show or vegetables from their gardens for the produce competition. There are craft shows and cooking contests." Her eyes shone with encouragement. "Each contestant may enter three items."

Polly pulled the strand of hair from her mouth. "What are *we* going to do?"

"Register for a ceramics class," Mother held up a board. "And Father cut wood so you can try your hand at carving."

During hot afternoons all summer, we enjoyed the air conditioning inside our home and diligently worked on our 4-H projects. We put the final touches on our crafts and entered them at the county fair. After the judging, Mother and I made our way past the food trucks, fair rides, and through the displays.

"Look, you have a third-place ribbon for your wood carving. Good work," Mother said.

I considered the judges to be very generous, considering all the visible scratches in the wood.

Valorie skipped up to my side. "Susan, we both received first place ribbons in ceramics."

But that wasn't my main interest. My pulse raced in anticipation as we entered the staging area for my final entry—the knitting section.

Mum Jenkins had spent hours teaching me to knit. So, all that summer, while my needles clicked and a variegated red, white, and blue poncho took shape, my memories had centered on her.

Mother and I entered the clothing items section. I stared at the ribbon pinned to my shawl and blinked back tears.

Mother gasped. "Purple. The highest prize anyone can receive at a county fair. You're qualified to re-enter your item at State." Her I'm-so-proud-of-you smile seemed to stretch from Cheney to Wichita.

I touched the gold lettering on the ribbon. *Here's to you, Mum Jenkins.*

August 1974, Beulah Camp in Wichita, Kansas

While attending my first missionary service, the speaker's account of God helping his family evangelize Alaskan Natives captivated me.

I sat on the edge of my seat, in rapt attention. What a fantastic idea! Imagine sending Christians to every corner of the world.

The missionary explained that evangelism was primarily the work of the Holy Spirit. The Holy Spirit gave the lost soul a sense of guilt, convicted them of their sin, and gave them confidence to believe in Jesus as their Savior. As a result of this newfound faith, Christ could help them overcome addictions such as alcoholism. Or overcome fear and find peace. Or learn to forgive and love others.

The tale of deliverance from the bondage of sin struck a chord in my heart. I bowed my head and whispered, *God, I want to be a missionary. Please make me a missionary.*

I had no special skills, I could only offer myself to God. If He could use me to help others, I was available.

One afternoon Mother joined me on the front steps. "Susan," she said, "we received a letter from your grandmother Goldie thanking us for adopting you. I thought you'd like to read it."

"Grandma Goldie?" She'd always intimidated me. I'd been so uncomfortable around her, and I couldn't imagine her doing such a thing as sending my new parents a thank-you note.

"She would be your father's mother."

"What does Grandma know about the adoption?"

"Read her letter and see." She handed it to me and turned to leave.

"Do you know where Marcus lives?" I asked.

"In Nova Scotia with your grandmother, Nan."

Grandma Nan. How I missed her. Even though Father's mother—my *new* grandmother—had lived with us, her recent death meant I hadn't really gotten to know her.

I settled in the crook of a large oak tree and unfolded the letter.

Dear Mr. and Mrs. Henley,

Thank you for doing what I could not do in my old age: raise my grandchildren. I praise God for sending them to a home where they are loved and taught the fear of the Lord. My parents died in the Halifax Explosion in December 1917. Without the gracious love of my Aunt Bertha, I, too, would have been sent to a state orphanage. Attached is the story of my adoption. Please share this with my grandchildren when you deem the time appropriate.

Lovingly,
Grandma Goldie

My Story, By Grandma Goldie:
December 1917, Halifax Explosion

On that day, mother and I were supposed to meet Aunt Bertha at her house then go choose a Christmas tree. I was so excited and determined to pick the fattest tree I could find. One with loads of branches.

Mother smoothed my hair and kissed me in the hallway of our home, then went outside to warm up the car. I was to wait there, already wearing my pretty coat with its gold buttons, until she came back to get me.

Bang! *The house vibrated and my eardrums rang. I shrank into the corner and buried my face in the crook of my arm. I'd never heard such a terrifying noise.*

Seconds later there was a blinding flash and the front door windowpanes imploded, sending a mixture of dust, smoke, and debris flying in all directions. Tiny shards of glass pricked the backs of my hands and embedded themselves in my skin.

I screamed, sprang up, and ran out onto the porch.

At the edge of the veranda, I stopped and rubbed my eyes. Trees, light posts, traffic signs, and power lines were strewn across yards and littered the street. The neighborhood was shattered and broken.

"Mummy. Where are you, Mummy?" I longed for the security of her loving embrace.

But she didn't answer, and I couldn't see her. I cinched my coat and descended the front steps.

A mother carrying the limp form of her baby ran screaming down the center of the road. A neighbor stood in the doorway of his house crying, "I'm blind! Someone please help me." Acrid smoke and the odor of explosives choked the air, and the wail of sirens told me something was terribly wrong.

My legs wobbled as I stumbled down the sidewalk. "Mummy. Mummy?" But the falling snow muffled my cries, and no one answered.

I wandered for several hours, blinded by the storm and disoriented because I couldn't see familiar landmarks. Giant snowflakes floated to the ground, blanketing the carnage with a soft layer of whiteness. As I struggled to step over the mounds of snow-covered debris, I grew so tired.

Then, I saw a dog huddling under the boughs of a pine tree. He lifted his head and barked.

"Good doggy," I said. "May I join you?" I crawled under the tree and snuggled next to the pup. I drifted to sleep beside him, remembering the many times mother had said to me, "Rest, dear. You'll feel better in the morning."

Aunt Bertha found me there under the tree and woke me. "Child, thank God I found you." She hugged me tightly and choked back tears. "Are you okay?"

I nodded. "Where's Mummy?"

"Dearie, you know your parents loved you."

I didn't understand, but my throat felt tight, and I was already sad.

"A ship in the harbor exploded, and many people died. Your mummy and daddy are in heaven."

My aunt wept, and I sobbed.

"There, there. Cry it out, dearie." Aunt Bertha smoothed my hair and kissed my forehead just as Mum had done. "You're my daughter now."

What I'd thought was a nightmare was actually true.

I laid Grandma Goldie's letter in my lap. Funny how threads connect us with the past. I wished I had known her better—she was the only one who seemed to notice or even acknowledge our adoption. Perhaps someday, I would return to Nova Scotia and learn more about her story, other things we had in common, and the disaster that claimed so many lives.

Susan Carter

CHAPTER TWENTY

Reconnection and Direction

December 1976, Cheney, Kansas
Susan

I loved being close to mother as she prepared our meals. She never used recipes, she simply threw in a pinch of this and a dash of that.

"How do you make *whatever*?" I often asked.

"I never write anything down," she'd say. "I keep tasting until it's right."

On one such afternoon, I was watching snow fall on the fields through the kitchen window, when the phone rang.

Mother stilled the rolling pin and shook a flour-coated hand in my direction. "Susan, get the phone."

I lifted the receiver with the calendar in hand, assuming the caller sought a babysitter. "Hello, this is Susan."

"Alright, sir, your party is on the line," the operator said. "You may go ahead with your call."

"He—hello? Susan? This is your father. Are you there?"

I clutched my sweater. Had I heard correctly? I pressed the phone against my ear. "Yes."

"How are you, love?" Dad's voice dripped with emotion.

His voice, a rich baritone with a Nova Scotian accent, rang in my ears. I'd thought I'd never again hear that sound.

"And your brothers?" Dad asked.

"Oh, they're fine." I struggled to swallow the lump in my throat. "And I'm fine, too." I turned to face the wall and kept my voice low, hoping Mother wouldn't overhear. "The boys are playing downstairs by the fire."

"Will you call them for me? Can I talk to them?" Dad's voice broke.

I blew out a long breath and stalled for time. *How can I politely wiggle out of this?* "Um ... I don't think that would be a good idea. I'd need to ask permission from my parents, and I'm pretty sure they'd say no."

"Yeah." His voice fell. "Okay. I miss you all terribly, dear. The holidays are hardest when you're away from family, eh? I just wanted to hear your voice ... Don't forget that I love you."

My heart pounded in my ears. *I'm talking with my dad. Oh, I have so much to share! But how does one reduce a million stories to three seconds?* Unshed tears stung my eyes. "Merry Christmas, Dad," I whispered.

"Remember, I love you." Dad drew a breath, then the line went dead.

I turned back around.

"Who was that?" Mother asked.

I looked away.

"Hope you didn't schedule anything for Thursday. Grandma is coming to help you sew winter pajamas."

"No." I searched Mom's face. "It, it was my birth

father. He called to wish everyone a Merry Christmas."

Her lips tightened. "Well, of all the nerve."

Mother threw down her towel and hurried out of the room.

I ran to my walk-in closet and shut the door. My refuge, a retreat I shared only with our cat, Mush. The cat purred contentedly in the large window, sunning himself. I sank onto the carpet beside Mush and stroked his soft fur.

Tears of gratitude soaked my cheeks. *Thank You, Lord, for the gift of hearing the love and longing in my father's voice. Thank You for the gift of knowing Dad's thoughts are with us this Christmas.*

Fall 1980, Cheney, Kansas

As a child living in the ghettos, I'd never dreamed of completing high school, let alone going to college. But after my adoption, I found the emotional energy to focus on my studies.

I viewed high school as a privilege and studied diligently, graduating with honors. High academic placement scores and letters of recommendation resulted in receiving a full scholarship from Friends University in Wichita, Kansas.

On enrollment day, the school counselor called our home. "Where's Susan? Why isn't she enrolling for class?"

My father found me lying on my bed, reading a book. "Honey, do you need a ride to Wichita?"

I had thought a lot about attending Friends and the generous scholarship. For years, I'd used my babysitting money to pay for weekly voice lessons at Friends.

During the last semester of my senior year, I'd asked my father's opinion of my choice to major in music. In reality, I was fishing for encouragement.

"I don't think you would make it," he said. "To succeed as a woman in the music world, you need two things: a fantastic voice and great legs." He gave me a sympathetic smile. "You have the legs, but not the voice."

All through high school I'd competed at the bi-weekly music competitions and consistently received the highest rating. I sang with my siblings at church and was often asked to sing solos. *Someone* thought my singing was okay.

My favorite singer was my father. I could sit for hours listening to him sing love songs to Mother, his golden tenor voice soaring above the record player. To receive his vote of approval would have been like receiving a membership badge to the musician's circle. His rejection stung—my singing was not up to par with his standards of excellence. But I chose to ignore the slam and instead focused on other benefits of attending Friends University.

"But I love the idea of attending Friends. And it's only a thirty-minute drive to Cheney, close enough to come home on weekends."

"Friends is a state university," Father said. "You'll have to stand alone in your faith and beware of teachers with worldly philosophies."

As I contemplated my father's warning, I realized I needed to look in a different direction. I needed a school where I would be encouraged to grow academically and spiritually. Somewhere far from home where I could spread my wings.

So, when my father came looking for me on registration day for Friends, I had an answer ready.

"I believe God is calling me to serve as a missionary.

To receive the proper training, I need to attend a Christian college. I've submitted an application for the spring semester at a Bible school in Florida."

Dad nodded—his way of showing he knew I'd made up my mind.

"Besides, I've technically only lived here for eight years. Now I'll have four more months in your care."

I could tell I hadn't taken my father by surprise. He'd probably known I'd take his advice and choose not to attend a secular college. My decision told him I was ready to leave home and embrace adulthood.

The following spring, I left for Bible college in Hobe Sound, Florida, with less than a hundred dollars in my pocket and trusting God to take care of me. That first semester, I received a music scholarship. My travels with the college public relations group covered my tuition, room, and board in the following years. I prayed over every financial need I had—laundry money, choir shoes, textbooks. As I learned to trust my heavenly Father to provide my needs, my confidence in prayer grew. God did hear and answer prayer. And he cared for little ol' me.

September 1982, Hobe Sound, Florida

The hot sun beat down on me, as I crossed the bridge and took the shortcut to class.

"Hey," a masculine voice said behind me. "Wait up, young lady. Let me carry your books."

"Alright," I said, determined to be as friendly as others I'd met at college. Making friends had been easy for me, so why not be a friend to another?

Long slender fingers reached for my textbooks as a lanky gentleman flashed me a brilliant smile.

I caught a whiff of his cologne and blushed.

He extended his hand. "Ken."

"Susan. Pleased to meet you."

"I hope you are."

The heat in my cheeks intensified as we fell in step.

"I saw you take the outreach bus Sunday afternoon."

"Yes, I go to the sugarcane camps and work with the children."

"Every week?" he asked.

"Whenever I'm not out with the choir."

He flashed another dazzling smile. "Mind if I join your team?"

From that point on, we were inseparable. I drank in the specialness of being wanted and admired. I was at a Christian college dating a guy who loved God. I trusted Ken not to hurt me, so I opened my heart to him and loved him without reservation.

April 1983

During a Sunday evening service in the spring semester of my sophomore year, the minister concluded his sermon by opening the altar for prayer. The urge to go forward quickly rose within me, and I yielded to it. "Is there something You want to tell me, Lord?" I prayed. "I'm listening."

It's time. Release the bitterness in your heart. Give those resentments to me. Forgive your birth parents, and I will heal your soul.

"Jesus, I'm not consciously holding onto bitterness." I thought I'd buried those hurts long ago.

Exactly.

"Lord, You see the hearts of men. You know me better than I know myself. Please cleanse my emotions from every trace of bitterness toward my birth parents. I am ready to surrender my past to You. I'm ready to be healed."

Intense sorrow, as I'd never before experienced, gripped my soul. Heart-wrenching sobs shook my body. I realized I did harbor anger toward my mother for leaving me. I did question God for allowing us to suffer at the hand of irresponsible adults. And I was bitter toward my birth parents. Rivers of tears streamed down my cheeks, cleansing away the pain, pent-up disappointment, and the *whys* that had lurked in the secret places of my memory.

One by one, the other seekers at the altar completed their prayers and quietly slipped away. The church custodian blew out the vanilla-scented candles and turned down the tabernacle lights, leaving me alone in the presence of God, my Heavenly Father.

Eventually, my sobs subsided. I thanked God for His faithfulness to speak to me. All sense of time evaporated as a spirit of worship and gratitude consumed my thoughts. I raised my face and hands toward heaven.

"I am unworthy of your forgiveness and love," I said aloud to God. "Thank You for making me your child. Thank You for your conviction and for showing me the bitterness hidden in the depths of my heart. I give all those hurts and disappointments to You."

As I communed with the Holy Spirit, waves of peace flooded my soul. God's enduring love bubbled within me like cool water from a spring. At that moment, I realized I was not only in God's presence with His glory surrounding me, but He was flooding my emotions with a love so intense, it physically hurt.

I wanted that moment to continue forever—loving God, sensing His divine presence. I felt like a new person, reborn all over again. Later, in the wee hours of the morning under a canopy of brilliant stars, I made my way back to my bunk in the dorm and fell into a sound sleep.

June 1983

I carefully packed the picnic in a wicker basket and covered it with a red and white checkered tablecloth. I wanted the date to be perfect. I had scouted the beaches all week, chosen the ideal spot, and gathered driftwood I'd hidden in the seagrass.

I sat on the bench in front of the girl's dorm and waited for Ken. He approached, holding his arm behind his back, then proudly handed me a bouquet.

"Black-eyed Susans. Your selection is perfect." As I took the stems, the flowers drooped. "I can't believe the florist sold you wilted flowers. What a shame."

Ken threw his head back and laughed. "Alright, I confess. Why waste twenty-five bucks on flowers when I can pick weeds from the ditch? Sorry. Guess I should have brought them in a container of water."

Was I not worth the twenty-five-dollar investment? No, I shouldn't think that way.

At the beach, Ken poked our crackling fire with a stick. A gentle breeze swept my hair back from my face. Hotdogs sizzled and waves crashed. Happiness saturated my being and soaked into my bones like the golden rays of the sunset reflected on the clouds above us.

I gazed adoringly at Ken. "What is there about me that caught your attention?"

"When I attended high school, I always wanted to date a cheerleader, but none of them gave me a second glance. When I came to Bible School all the beautiful and talented girls were in the choir."

"You chose me because I sing?"

"Get serious."

I drew in the sand and waited.

"It's more than that. I'd never date a girl I couldn't envision marrying."

Marriage? I was so delighted, I almost giggled. Ken was thinking of marriage. So was I.

After dinner, we walked along the surf with sandpipers racing ahead of us. I brushed my fingers against Ken's. "You may take my hand."

"Nope, can't. When I prayed about dating, the Lord told me to keep our relationship platonic. That's the deal."

"And what does that mean?"

"Bottom line—no touching."

My jaw dropped. I stood by a young man with the inner fortitude and self-control to shun the natural inclination to hold his girlfriend's hand. His standard of moral purity and restraint amazed me. I thought guys of this caliber only existed in Grace Livingston Hill novels.

God, how did I rate getting a prize like Ken? Thank You for the care and love You are showing to me through this godly gentleman. Make me worthy of his love and devotion.

July 1983

That summer I sang soprano in a ladies' trio, traveling to churches and youth camps representing the college. Our journeys took us to Toronto. The night before the border crossing into Canada, I called home to Kansas and spoke with Mother and Father.

"Our next stop is Toronto, and I'm staying with Marcus. I hope to see my birth parents, but the thought of seeing them—well, it's been ten years. I'm nervous." I sensed the tension in the silence on the other end of the line. Despite my waning courage, I plunged on. "I just wanted you to know that if I do get to see my birth parents it won't diminish my love for you. I'll love you forever. You'll always be my parents."

Father cleared his throat. "We hope you will have the wisdom to rely on God during this visit and not tax your emotions with ties to the past. Your greatest peace is knowing those ties are broken—entirely severed."

A tightness dominated my father's tone. I envisioned teardrops cascading down my mother's cheeks. I understood their fear—that's why I called them.

"You are forever a part of us now," Dad continued, "with an unbreakable bond in Christ. That's a bond blood relatives cannot interfere with or break. Don't let anyone saddle you with guilt or responsibility that isn't yours. You have a stable present and a glorious future in Christ. You owe the past nothing."

Once again, I reassured them of my love. Still, it hurt that my father thought I should forget the history woven into my identity—my biological family. I deeply loved my adoptive parents. Their love and sensitivity had filled the emotional gaps left from years of neglect in my childhood.

From my adopted mother, I learned what I imagined many mothers share with their daughters. She taught me to sew, cook, clean house, garden, can green beans and peaches, and how to care for children. Most of all, she taught me the subtle nuances of behaving like a lady. She guided me to dress modestly, carry myself with poise, practice grace, and be attentive to the needs of others. More than anyone else, my mother shaped my life. I was immensely grateful to her.

At the same time, the Holy Spirit constrained me to pray for my birth parents' salvation. Didn't the Bible teach us to forgive our offenders and offer them unconditional love? I counted this desire to connect with my birth parents as a gift from God.

The following morning, our tour bus drove across the bridge into Canada. I expected to feel joy, but Ontario no longer felt like home.

Later, Marcus ushered me into his apartment, where I found my birth Mum sitting in a corner recliner. While I'd looked forward to seeing her, I wondered if she would be the same or if time had changed her. The ten years we'd been apart felt like a lifetime. When I left Toronto before, I was a confused little girl. Now I had returned as a confident adult.

"Hey there, Suzie-Q." Mum used my pet name as though no time had elapsed since we'd seen each other.

We exchanged an awkward hug. The light scent of lily perfume brought back a million memories: times we shared bedtime hugs, nighttime trips to the corner store to buy chocolate, and snuggling on the couch watching soap operas.

I turned away to hide my tears, while Marcus and Mum eased into a relaxed banter.

Sitting on the sofa with my legs curled beneath me, I studied her mannerisms, quirks, and way of saying things. Yes, I remembered how her little finger pointed upward when she held her teacup and how she tilted her head when she laughed.

A shock ran through me as I realized—something or someone had hurt my mother. The smile she wore wasn't reflected in the dark seriousness of her eyes. Had she always been that way?

"I want to see Dad," I blurted.

Mum and Marcus exchanged apprehensive glances.

"Why do you want to see him?" Marcus asked. "He's probably drunk."

"Do you know where he lives?"

Marcus nodded. "Last time I visited his place, I asked him to stop drinking, and he gave me a black eye."

"I still want to see him."

The following morning, Marcus and I rode the streetcar to Dad's place, a flat on the second floor above a store on Queen Street. My brother rapped on the door, five sharp knocks, and stepped backward. The sadness in his eyes said *Don't say I didn't warn you.*

Heavy footsteps descended on the stairs. I bit my lower lip and moved behind my brother.

The door burst open. "What are you doing here?" Dad scowled at Marcus.

Marcus stepped to one side, revealing me.

My father froze in apparent shock. Then for long moments he searched my face. He reached and drew me into a bone-crushing hug and quivered with emotion. "Susan, my dear, I knew you'd come back. I knew you'd come back." Finally, he released me. "Come in and visit for a bit?"

Dad's embrace and joy at seeing me brought an immediate measure of healing to me. Once again, I was reassured of his love. Once again, I confirmed the same to him.

We ascended the narrow staircase to his modest apartment and entered the kitchen.

"Let me put on a pot of tea," Dad said.

Marcus and I sat at the metal table.

"You look good, dear," Dad said.

"Thank you. Listen, we can't stay long. I'm traveling with a group from college and need to meet up with them in an hour. I just wondered if I could spend time with you on my next visit."

His eyes glistened. "I'd love that, dear. Just send me the dates, and I'll be all yours."

We finished our tea and rose to leave.

I hugged my father's neck. "Bye, Dad." Even though my father had abandoned us, he, too, had been scarred by his choice.

"Don't say goodbye, dear," Dad's eyes revealed his sadness and brokenness.

"See you soon."

"Yes, we'll be talkin'."

"I love you," I said.

Dad blinked back his tears and waved.

I walked away aching to introduce Dad to Jesus, the healer of damaged souls. I prayed God would give me that opportunity.

Susan Carter

CHAPTER TWENTY-ONE

Answered Prayer and Heartbreak

June 1984, Toronto, Ontario
Susan

I once again traveled with the college trio. As before, our itinerary took us to eastern Ontario.

When I stayed with Marcus the previous summer, several cousins had promised to attend the service to hear me sing, but no one had showed. My brother called during the pre-service spaghetti dinner to tell me everyone had canceled. The sting of rejection had killed my appetite. I left the meal and sought solace in the back seat of the college van, weeping through dinner.

My father had said he would come to hear me sing this time. But knowing he'd have to drive three hours to attend the service, and based on previous experience with my cousins, I didn't expect him to show up. When he entered the church foyer, joy took my breath away. As we sang the first song, his face beamed. Never before had Dad heard me sing. I wanted him to know this side of my life. I wanted to make him proud.

After the concert, I had a few days free to spend with

Dad. On the ride back to Toronto, conversation flowed freely.

"I don't normally ask for favors," Dad said, "but if you're able, will you sing for my funeral?"

"Are you dying?" The words stuck in my throat.

"The doc gave me a defibrillator. My days are limited. I have two years, at best."

"What's wrong with you?"

"I've had several minor heart attacks. The defibrillator will shock my heart and keep me alive. But it also limits my days."

I bit my lip. *Don't cry. Focus on today.*

We packed beautiful memories into the time we spent together. We visited the CN Tower, rode the ferry, and fed the pigeons at the City Hall Plaza. Dad gave me a tour of the places most meaningful to him. He shared with me how after he lost us children, he quit his job and became homeless. He spent his days begging on street corners, drinking to drown his sorrows, and endured miserable nights curled in a cardboard box in a forsaken alley or an abandoned building. That he now held down a job and had his own place was an accomplishment.

At one point, we stood by a public fountain where he had bathed during his homeless days. As I ran my hand through the cool fountain water, I thought back to those summer nights in Kansas when I had slipped out of bed and knelt by my window. Twinkling stars seemed to poke holes in the darkness, and a warm breeze caressed my skin. In the silence of the night, I prayed for my dad. I pictured him sad, and alone, and laying destitute in a dark alley.

"God, have mercy on my dad," I often whispered. "Turn his thoughts to You. Please send someone to share the Gospel with him and bring him hope."

We drove to an abandoned building, and dad stopped in front of it.

"I used to sleep here with my drinking buddy," he said. "One night, a fire destroyed the building and killed my friend."

"Where were you?" I asked.

"Strange thing is, that night, I slept on a park bench. When I returned the next morning, fire trucks lined the street." Dad's voice broke.

"How terrible."

"That's when I left behind the life in the gutter and found a job as a taxi driver. Before long, I had enough to pay the deposit on my apartment."

"I'm sorry about your friend."

"Where to now, Do-Bee?" Dad asked.

"I'd like to see the apartment on Queen Street where we used to live. "

"I don't go to that neighborhood anymore. But I'll take you."

A tangible silence filled the car as we drove through our old neighborhood and parked across from our old home.

"We made sweet memories here, Dad. Remember all the nights we stayed up late working puzzles?" I whispered.

Dad's eyes glistened.

"But ... we had tough times, too," I said.

Dad gripped the steering wheel.

I swallowed the lump in my throat and plowed on. "Those times are past and forgiven. I have prayed for you all these years. God has great plans for you. Chapters of your life are still unwritten. Jesus wants to fill those pages with His love, mercy, forgiveness, and grace. Why not let Him write the ending?"

I withdrew a photo from my purse and handed it to

my father.

"Smells like perfume," he said.

"A trick my girlfriends taught me."

Dad flipped over the picture and read the inscription.

I believe in you. I am praying for you. Forever, your daughter, Susan.

He turned the key in the ignition, his chin quivering. "This tour is over."

I knew my words had touched my dad's heart, but I didn't want to push. So, I backed off to let the Holy Spirit work.

August 1984, Hobe Sound, Florida

I returned to college for my senior year. Every day while walking to class, I stopped by the post office and checked my mail. Usually, the box was empty. But in October, I found a letter from my birth father.

That day, I skipped class and returned to my room to open the envelope in private.

My Dear Susan,

I don't know what I'm going to say, but I hope you'll understand the feelings of my heart. To start with, I no longer live in Ontario. I left three months ago, the same day I had my last drink of alcohol.

My life, especially the past few years, has been defined by guilt, remorse, pride, resentfulness, fear, self-pity, and the list goes on and on.

As a youngster, my mother took me to Sunday school and

church. I guess I always knew God existed. I realize He never left me; I rejected Him.

While taking that last drink, I cried out to God, not with words, but from the depths of my soul, "God, please help me."

Remember last summer when we were up in the CN Tower? The whole time something pulled at my heart, eh? I didn't want to tell you or admit to myself that God was speaking to me. In the car, when you asked if I could feel the Spirit of God—I cried because of the overwhelming guilt that filled my soul. I wanted to ask you to pray for me, but I didn't. Rather, on the night you left, I walked to the store to buy beer and numb my conscience.

Now, to stay sober, I have to be honest with myself at least once, right? It hurts something awful to remember how I drank instead of being a father to you and your brothers and sisters. (Man, just the thought makes me crave a drink). Many times, I have tried to sober up on my own, but I failed.

This year I joined Alcoholics Anonymous. I opened my heart to let God take over, and my life is better for it. Now each day when I wake up, I ask God to set my path, and in the evening, before I go to sleep, I thank God for His help. (Every day I do not drink is a good day). If I have a problem, I turn it over to God.

Susan, after all this time, I have found a new way to live. I know there is a God, and I know He is with me.

I carry the picture you gave me in my wallet. When my friends from AA read what you wrote on the back, they say, "Dave, God has answered her prayers."

Dear, what I'm saying is, after all this time, your God is my God.

Love, your father,
Dave

I fell to my knees and wept for joy. Over and over, I

thanked my Heavenly Father for His mercies and His faithfulness to answer prayer. Reading my father's clear testimony of salvation brought great comfort to my heart.

August 1985, Lorain, Ohio

While I was away at college, my parents moved to Ohio. Ken and I consistently talked of marriage. Although he didn't officially propose, I presumed we had an understanding. Midway through my senior year, I returned home to Ohio to prepare for our wedding. Emptying my savings, I fell into preparations with a vengeance. Purchasing the material for the dresses. Addressing the invitations. Planning the wedding service and booking the photographer. By the time Ken came to visit, one chore remained—premarital counseling.

Linking arms, Ken and I entered the church and made our way to the pastor's office. The minister directed us to sit in the leather chairs facing his desk.

"Do you love each other?"

I threw my head back and laughed. *We're getting married. Hello!*

The pastor clicked his pen, waiting for an answer.

"Yes," I said.

Ken nodded.

"Do you ever wonder if there's anyone better suited for you?"

I shook my head. *We're perfect together.* Same goals, same priorities, same values. Yes, marriage required minor adjustments, but everyone faced those. We were wonderfully matched.

Ken leaned forward, planting his elbows on his knees. "I love Susan. I do. She's a beautiful person inside and out. But I'm not sure she'll fulfill my desires. I'm afraid I won't be content with her flat chest. I don't want to have a miserable marriage. Honestly, I can live without her. Bottom line, I'd like a year to explore other options."

I pressed a trembling hand to my burning cheeks. Ken had told me breast size didn't matter. He'd said I was perfect.

My world reeled to a stop as shock went to humiliation and grief. *He's changed his mind.*

The pastor lifted his phone and dialed. "Honey, I need you here immediately." He dropped the receiver into its cradle, then he stood. "I wouldn't touch this wedding with a ten-foot pole," he mumbled.

Ken sighed, visibly relieved.

The man I loved and trusted with my heart had rejected me, and his excuse was the size of my breasts? I fled, stumbling through the maze of hallways to the women's prayer room. Inside, I dove for a wooden bench and collapsed.

Dizzy. I'm so dizzy.

I pressed my back against the cool cinderblock wall, seeking stability. In the darkness, I focused on the dim light surrounding a mural of the globe.

Breathe. Just breathe.

This new pain flattened me as much of my childhood trauma had done.

I don't know how long I sat there alone. At some point, the pastor's wife arrived. She wrapped her arm around my shoulder and covered my clenched hands in hers.

"Father," she prayed.

Above the roar of heartbeats ringing in my ears, I heard her calm, steady voice.

"In this moment of pain, I ask you to undergird Susan with your divine love and sustain her as she moves into the unknown ..."

Breathe. Breathe. Breathe. As she continued praying, the coldness of being abandoned passed through my veins.

When the pastor's wife finished praying and verified Ken had left the building, she accompanied me back to my apartment. I spent the afternoon racking my brain for missed clues to Ken's disillusion.

That evening, I called my sister, Polly. "I can't believe this is happening," I sobbed. "Exactly two months before our wedding! This afternoon, I canceled our appointment with the baker." A fresh round of tears rolled down my cheeks.

"Why did he wait until now to bail?"

"We've been in a long-distance relationship for several months, right?" I reached for another Kleenex. "I'm working full-time to pay for the wedding while he completes college. Maybe he got to looking around and found someone else? I don't knooow."

"Oh, you poor thing! Ken has lost a treasure. He'll have to look a long time to find someone as kind and loving as you. It'll take him a lifetime to recover, if he ever does."

I told myself I'd rather be single than live with someone who didn't treasure and love me. But in my hour of excruciating pain, rationalizations were of no comfort. Would I ever find love?

To lift my spirits and redefine my identity, I switched my dress style from romantic frills and bows to straight-lined business suits, and my perfume from cheap to expensive.

I couldn't shake the rejection. The depression that settled over me became an impenetrable despair—a consuming grief. I hadn't suffered so since losing Mum Jenkins.

Loneliness took hold. Ken had been my best friend. My confidant. My soon-to-be mate for life. My misery grew into thoughts that I didn't belong anywhere and would never belong to anyone. Once again, I was unwanted. During the day, I experienced sharp stomach pains. My nights were equally restless.

I recalled hearing sermons linking depression with spiritual shallowness. I dared not share my battle with depression with my church family, fearing they would consider me spiritually shallow. I convinced myself I simply needed to spend more time in prayer. But the more I prayed, the more I believed my prayers circled the universe, unheard. Month after torturous month, dark depression plagued me.

Spring 1986

My days had become nothing but drudgery, and I was desperate for relief. Any relief.

I drove southeast from Ohio toward the coast. I arrived in the wee hours of the morning, found an empty parking lot, and slid my vehicle into the darkest corner. I tossed my keys under the front seat, not caring they'd be challenging to find.

After all, I wouldn't need them anymore.

I headed for the steep embankment, passing under a dim, humming pole light. I threw my shoes into the seagrass. Following the sound of crashing waves and the smell of saltwater, I shuffled down the sandy path toward the shore. Beneath my feet, shifting sand changed to a wet, hard-packed surface. Then, the cold surf lapped at my toes.

Where was the horizon? The sea and the sky melded together into an endless curtain of blackness. I had assumed there would be stars and moonlight. *Wrong.*

Soon the water reached my ankles. Thunder rumbled in the distance. I shivered as a chilly breeze swept back my hair.

Waves crashed in front of me, slapping against my legs, splashing water up to my waist. No. This wasn't the right spot. Too close to the beach access path.

I retreated from the water, turned and walked south, putting distance between me and the parking lot. I glanced backward—darkness enveloped the shoreline. Once more, the ocean loomed before me. I pushed knee-deep into the water, then paused again, grasping for courage.

I had imagined there would be boats bobbing in the water, marking the horizon. I planned to use the lights from those boats as directional markers, guiding me farther and farther from the shore. But the brewing storm meant the ships were anchored at the docks, leaving the water deserted.

Alone. So completely alone in my anguish and crushing despair.

Wade into the deep. Swim forever. No retreat. Yield to the ocean's depths.

I plunged deeper into the waves, water spraying my face. An inner voice whispered, *Shouldn't you pray and commit your soul to God?*

I paused and returned to the shore. I sat with my knees drawn into my chest, despite the sand fleas.

"There's a reason he dumped her. I can't picture her as a pastor's wife." I imagined the whispers of others. Hadn't Ken's pastor told him my messy childhood disqualified me from being a pastor's wife, and he should look for someone who'd been brought up in the church?

I decided I wouldn't defend myself to anyone wondering about the broken engagement. It was no one's business but mine that Ken had publicly humiliated me. Others could fabricate all the stories they wished. I would never disclose the details.

I remembered the advice of a well-meaning relative. "You need a fresh start. Move to California and disassociate yourself from the church world."

Isolate myself from the body of Christ but try to live as a Christian? Was that possible? My heartache and sorrows from childhood had taught me the hellishness of life without God. Lightning flashed on the horizon, and thunder rumbled louder, closer. A gust of chilling wind whipped sand into my eyes and across my cheeks. The surf slapped against the rocks along the shore, still beckoning.

Hot rivulets of tears coursed down my cheeks and a ripple of terror passed through me. If I ended my life, would God forgive me?

I had known the presence of God. He had answered my prayers, provided for my needs, and healed the brokenness of my youth. Where was He tonight?

"God, please help me!" I called into the darkness. "Father, I don't know the way out. You know my situation. I see no future for me on this earth, and I can't walk away from You. Please forgive me for what I am about to do."

You belong to me. God's Spirit whispered to my soul.

I remembered Jeremiah 29:11—"For I know the thoughts that I think toward you, says the Lord, thoughts of peace and not of evil, to give you a future and a hope."

I sobbed so hard my body shook. "But I can't go on alone."

Then Joshua 1:9—"Be strong and of good courage; do not be afraid, nor be dismayed, for the LORD your God *is* with you wherever you go."

I talked with God all night, wrestling with Him over my pain. Eventually, a faint line of gray appeared on the horizon, sandpipers chased one another into the surf, and the mourning doves cooed softly in the trees along the embankment. With the breaking of the dawn, despite not experiencing relief, I rose and brushed the sand from my clothes.

I knew what to tell myself—*In myself, I am nothing; but in Christ, I am a child of God.* But even after driving safely home to my apartment, the profound sadness in my soul persisted. Most nights I sobbed into my pillow, soaking it with my tears.

One night, I cried out, "Oh, Lord, I can't take any more of this pain! Please, hold me."

I lay there drained of all emotional strength. Then, a soft light seemed to fill the room. In my darkest hour, God wrapped the sweet warmth of his loving arms around me.

Soon, a welcome peace filled my soul and calmed my distress. The burden of sadness miraculously lifted. I stopped crying.

I flipped my pillow to the dry side and drifted into a deep, restful sleep. When I woke the next morning, the darkness and depression that had dominated my life for six months was gone.

CHAPTER TWENTY-TWO

Fresh Start

Summer 1986, Lorain, Ohio
Susan

The leadership team of my home church chose me as their new church secretary, and no one was more surprised than I was. One particular day after working two hours on the church bulletin, I was no closer to completing the job than when I started. I clicked the keys of the Smith Corona typewriter, pausing to reach for more Wite-out, then crumpled the practice bulletin and inserted a fresh sheet into the typewriter.

"Having a rough day?" a female voice asked.

I turned to see the organist standing in the doorway. "Challenging," I said with a smile.

"Technical skills can be learned."

I nodded. "How may I help you?"

"My sister and I own an antique shop. We are the ones who furnished your apartment."

"Oh, thank you. I love the round oak table in the kitchenette."

"We hoped you would."

"So, what can I do for you today?"

"There is a boutique next door to our store. Tonight, the owner is having a private sale. She sells business suits, fancy dresses with lace collars and pearl buttons, and all sorts of luxurious accessories. We want to take you out for a Mexican dinner, and afterward, we'll all go to the sale."

"It's sweet of you to think of me," I said. "But even at half price, I can't afford those clothes."

She cleared her throat. "I knew you'd say that. We're asking you to explore the shop and give us a selection of five outfits. We will select one of the five to give you, and we'll foot the bill."

"Oh my! That's way too generous."

"As church secretary, you represent us. You need to dress the part. We hope you'll accept our gift."

My heart burst with gratitude for this act of kindness.

Later that evening, I drove home with boxes of silk blouses, matching skirts, cashmere sweaters, and coordinating accessories piled in my back seat. I felt like a princess in a fairy tale. The ladies purchased all five outfits. What kind of friends did that? I bowed my head and thanked God for the elegant wardrobe.

August 1986, Cincinnati, Ohio

By God's grace, I entered the fall semester at God's Bible School in Cincinnati. God used the job experience and the gift of clothing I'd received in Lorain to provide for the next season of my life. I was blessed to participate in the student work program and serve as secretary for the Christian

Service department.

I was at my desk, typing away, when a young man walked in.

"I'm Gareth," he said.

"Susan."

He held up his Christian Service report.

"Basket." I motioned to the container on the edge of my desk, then returned to my work.

But I couldn't ignore my racing heart. When Gareth had looked at me with his deep blue eyes, he seemed to gaze into my soul. It was as if he already knew me and *liked* me. Kindness had radiated from his countenance. His seemingly unassuming personality reminded me of my saintly adopted mother.

The following day, I lingered outside the cafeteria until Gareth came for lunch. Then I took my place behind him in line.

"How's your day, Gareth?" I asked.

"Hello, Susan."

He seemed nervous. "I'll be visiting your downtown mission this weekend," I said. "What time do you gather the children?"

"We start at nine. You can skip that part. It's not always pleasant traipsing through the ghettos." Color rose in his cheeks.

"As Christian Service secretary, I need to write a report for each of the inner-city missions. I like to be thorough. You don't mind if I come earlier, do you?"

"No, of course, come." He pulled at his collar. "It's just, well, there are rats and uncomfortable situations. A fancy lady like you … might feel out of place."

Rats? I must remember to never visit the ghettos alone. I wiped my sweaty palms on my skirt. "I'll handle it," I said.

November 1986, Cincinnati, Ohio

The inner-city mission students gathered for their annual Thanksgiving banquet. As the guest speaker, I stood behind the podium and surveyed the crowd. My gaze landed on Gareth. His confused expression revealed his thoughts: *What tales of adversity could Susan possibly share?*

As I told my story of deliverance from poverty, Gareth's face seemed to glow with admiration. I feared he might give me a standing ovation.

After the banquet, Gareth stood beside me. "Susan," he spoke my name with reverence. "I believe God has a special plan for your life. I have written your name on my prayer list and pledge to pray for you daily, as long as I live."

Caught off guard, I laughed nervously. During our conversations, I'd learned he was from Key West, Florida. "How exactly did you come to this college?" I found I wanted to know everything about him.

"Honestly? I was sitting on a seawall flipping through a magazine from my parents' alma mater. Saltwater lapped at my feet and splashed onto the ledge beside me—have you ever been to Key West? The water is as clear as glass. In the canal behind our house, you'll see angel fish, barracuda, stingray ..." His voice trailed off and his face took on a far-away look.

"So why did you come north? Why Cincinnati?"

"I'd hoped to one day attend college and prepare to be a missionary. The church I attended back home served as the center of a world missionary outreach."

"Go on." I almost couldn't believe the coincidence

that his dreams aligned so easily with mine. *Lord, what exactly are you doing by crossing our paths?*

"I completed the application form and sent it in on a whim. Maybe I'd get in for next spring, you know? Then a student recruiter called and invited me to participate in their work scholarship program. I packed my bags and landed at Lunken Airport a few days later."

"That's ... that's amazing." I remembered how God had moved me and my siblings from Canada to Kansas. How He'd directed my path to Florida, and eventually Cincinnati. Yes, there had been heartache, but looking back, I clearly saw God's hand.

"That first week in the boys' dorm, I overheard a group of guys talking about the new Christian Service secretary."

My pulse quickened. *Me?* Did he mean me? Inside, I was dying to know what was said, but ...

"They were all anxious to turn in their Christian Service reports and check you out," he continued, as if reading my mind. "The consensus was you're a looker they all hoped was eligible. No disrespect, mind you. Just that you'd be a prize to any guy who caught your eye. I admit, I was curious. So, I climbed the stairs of the admin building to turn in my report."

He paused, and I all but held my breath, needing to hear what he thought of me. He must have seen that need reflected in my eyes.

"When I backed out of your office, I thought, *She's gorgeous. Those dark eyes and brown hair. And those expensive clothes? Yup. Guarantee she's an only child of a wealthy businessman.*"

"Well," I said. "Now you know that's not true."

"I guess not."

Gareth was so refreshingly transparent. I wasn't sure I'd ever met anyone like him. His friendship became a healing balm to my broken sense of self-worth. I valued his gift of unabashed admiration more than an elaborate bouquet.

May 1987

The week before summer break, the school hosted a revival. I sang with the choir on the evening of the final service. When the moderator dismissed the choir, I went directly to the cafeteria to raid the cooler. I found Gareth and his maintenance co-workers making turkey sandwiches.

Gareth joined me at a table in the far corner of the dining hall. "So, what are your summer plans?"

"I'm flying to Toronto the day after tomorrow for my brother's college graduation. Would you happen to know of anyone who could give me a ride to the airport?"

"I'd be happy to take you."

"You're sure it's not a bother?"

He smiled. "It's no problem whatsoever. Just tell me where and when."

Gareth had shown kindness to me over and over. Once, he'd noticed liquid pooling under my car. Not knowing if I'd agree to let him do the repairs, he bought the necessary parts, then searched the campus to find me practicing piano in the Music Hall. I couldn't help smiling as he approached, then I noticed he held an oil filter.

"Your car's leaking oil," he said. "I wonder if you'd permit me to fix it?"

"Yes." I didn't try to hide the joy his thoughtfulness

brought me. "And thank you."

Consequently, even though Gareth didn't have a car, I knew if he told me he'd give me a ride to the airport, he'd find a way to do it. He tried renting a vehicle, but the rental company required a credit card and wouldn't accept cash. So, the next day he spoke to his boss at the college and got permission to use one of the school's vehicles.

We rode in the van, Gareth steering into interstate traffic. "Say, would it be alright if I wrote to you over the summer?"

"You're welcome to write. But I'm spending the summer with relatives in Texas, and I'll be working full-time. Can't promise I'll have time to answer."

Gareth sagged against the driver's door and turned his eyes to the road.

I could tell I'd hurt his feelings, and I felt bad for that, especially after his generosity in taking me to the airport. But the break-up with Ken had taught me to be cautious. I wanted someone who was ready for a serious relationship.

June 1987, Boyd, Texas

I kissed Mother on the cheek and set my luggage inside the door. My parents had moved from Ohio to Texas two years prior after Dad accepted a teaching position close to Dallas. A gorgeous bouquet on the dining room table filled the air with the aroma of fresh-cut flowers.

"Dad bought you roses for your anniversary," I said. "How sweet."

Mother's eyes twinkled. "Oh, those aren't for me. The

card is addressed to you."

"Seriously? I'm not even dating anyone."

I snatched the envelope from the center of the bouquet, withdrew the card, and scanned the message.

I love you, Gareth.

I struggled to find my voice. "It's from a classmate."

Mother said nothing, but her knowing smile spoke volumes.

Later, alone in my room, thoughts whirled through my brain. What possessed Gareth to declare his love for me even though I had discouraged him from writing? Was I ready to jump into a new romance? The pain of my broken engagement still stung. That wound still bled at times.

I marveled at Gareth's courage and candor. Easing into the armchair by my bed, I folded my hands. *Could it be this man desired a serious relationship?* I laughed out loud at the surprise of joy welling within me. Gareth was looking for a lifelong companion, and he was choosing me.

I wrote Gareth a long letter, encouraging further correspondence. For the remainder of the summer, we exchanged weekly letters. This new, budding love began to heal my wounded heart. Gareth's tender words soothed me, restored my confidence, and revitalized my dreams.

Fall 1987, Cincinnati, Ohio

The college campus buzzed with student arrivals.

I found Gareth standing by the fishpond outside the chapel.

"Hey, Susan. Great to see you made it back." He

seemed as anxious to see me as I was to see him.

"Hi! Great to see you. I have a feeling this is going to be a memorable year."

Gareth drew in a breath, held it, then exhaled. "Say, what do you have planned for Saturday afternoon? Do you know how to roller skate?"

"Yes. And I'd love to." Our first real date.

Over the next few weeks, I learned Gareth had indeed been watching and hoping to woo me from the moment we first met.

He thought I carried myself with poise. How thankful I was my mother had taught me manners and how to behave like a lady.

He thought I was beautiful and intelligent. He'd even searched the dean's list to see if my name was there. How grateful I was for Mum Jenkins and teachers who had helped me discover I could learn.

When given the opportunity, he'd purposely sought me out in the chapel or lunchroom—our paths hadn't habitually crossed by chance.

He'd kept his intent and feelings so well-hidden, I hadn't considered several random, anonymous notes of encouragement left in my mailbox had been penned by him. I hadn't known he'd been the one to include a hundred dollars in one of those notes "for textbooks."

I'd thrown him quite a curveball when I left for Texas and made no commitment to write back all summer. So, he'd called his brother, who had a credit card, and enlisted his help in ordering the flowers.

"You know, I've kept my promise to pray for you every day," he said one evening.

And I knew it was true.

Two months after we started officially dating, Gareth booked a river cruise for my birthday. The lights of the Cincinnati skyline came into view as we rounded the bend on the Ohio River. Gareth placed his arm around my waist and drew me close. We leaned over the riverboat railing, listening to the waves against the hull and show tunes from the band below deck. Oblivious to the chill in the autumn air, my body warmed at his nearness.

He lifted my chin and looked deeply into my eyes. "I want to spend my life with you."

"Is that a proposal?" I'd wondered when he would ask. Hadn't he already declared his love when he sent the roses?

"You could call it that."

"I won't *call it that.* You have to ask properly."

"Susan, will you marry me?"

I raised my lips to his. "Yes. A thousand times yes."

CHAPTER TWENTY-THREE

New Beginnings

March 1988, Cincinnati, Ohio
Susan

I stood on a wooden platform and gripped the splintered post at my side. Above me, Jesus hung on a cross, slowly scanning the faces of the crowd. His gaze lingered on a woman on the edge of the stone path. I followed His gaze and saw Madeline, my birth mother.

What did Jesus see in her? I saw a broken, bewildered, and wretched soul. Her life, bruised and battered by the sinful choices she'd made. Battle scars marred her face, and a long shadow of past regrets threatened to rob her future.

Jesus looked on her with eyes filled with holy love and unfathomable pity. As I studied Jesus, conviction gripped my soul. Who was I to condemn my mother or to withhold compassion from her? Because of Jesus' sacrifice on the cross, the hope of redemption is hers, as well as mine ...

I awoke with a start. A profound sense of love for Mum settled over me. The spiritual indifference I'd felt toward her was replaced with genuine compassion and a commitment to pray for her as I had for my father.

March 1988, Toronto, Ontario

Gareth and I traveled to Toronto to meet Marcus's fiancée. My biological family would be there, and I was overjoyed to introduce Gareth to them as *my* fiancé. My birth mother met us at the door of Marcus' home.

I hugged Mum and kissed her cheek. Then I turned to Gareth. "I would like to introduce you to my mother."

Mum put her arm around my waist, and we walked up the stairs into the living room. "Would you like a sneak peek at the bride's wedding gown?"

"Will Stacey mind?"

"No, I already asked."

Once we were alone in the master bedroom, Mum turned to face me. Knowing she didn't waste words, I paid careful attention.

"I am so sorry I left you. If I could do everything over, I would do it differently. Please, can you ever forgive me?"

"Yes. I forgive you." I threw my arms around her.

When we emerged from the bedroom, Mum joined my grandmother Nan on the living room couch. "Ok, Mum. Susan and I had our little talk. You can stop worrying now."

I sensed that Nan's urging had prompted the apology. But Mum's tone, countenance, and demeanor conveyed her sincerity. Her apology soothed yet another wound in my slowly healing heart.

I went to pick up Thomas at the airport.

"Hello, Thomas," I said. "I can't say I expected to see you here." To my knowledge, I was the only one who had reconnected with our Canadian relatives.

"Marcus invited me," Thomas said. "I figured it's time to meet the family. The last time I saw our parents was when they came to see me at the hospital when my leg was broken. Remember?"

"I remember."

Marcus and Dave, our birth father, waited at the baggage claim for us. Marcus hadn't been home when I spoke with Mum and Nan. I hugged Marcus, while Thomas shook hands with our dad.

"Oh, for crying out loud," Marcus said. "You're family."

Dad chuckled and embraced Thomas.

The weekend with Marcus flew by as we made simple memories together enjoying backyard cookouts, playing board games, laughing, and crying. That Sunday evening, our luggage sat by the door, ready for our return trip to the airport. We sat around the dining room table, sipping one last tea, and delaying goodbyes.

"You're all invited to my wedding in May," Marcus said. "Then we'll travel to Texas in June for Susan's wedding."

"I'll be there," Dad said.

"No ... no, truly," I said. "I wouldn't expect you to come. It's too far."

Dad winked. "Well, I *am* invited, right?"

Marcus and Thomas quieted, tensely awaiting my answer.

I twisted my wristwatch. "I'm already pretty stressed over the details. There are so many I have no control over."

Marcus rolled his eyes.

"Everyone's invited to my wedding," Thomas said.

"When's that?" Marcus asked.

Thomas laughed. "Gotta find the gal first."

I appreciated Thomas deflecting the tension. I shuddered to think of the added stress if I had two fathers waiting to walk me down the aisle on my wedding day.

August 1988, Cincinnati, Ohio

We'd been married a mere two months when we paid cash for a Dodge Colt from a friend. Gareth immediately set about changing the oil and found the engine coated with gunk. My husband took a week off work, suffered immense frustration, and spent hundreds of dollars on that car. Once Gareth rebuilt the engine, the Colt ran like a champ.

But bitterness toward our friends troubled my heart. "They should never have sold it to us."

"Some guys don't know how to maintain their vehicles," Gareth said.

"At the very least they should refund the cost of repairs."

"Now, dear, I think we should pay a hundred dollars of their school bill." Gareth placed his hand on my shoulder.

My jaw dropped. "You're kidding."

"I'm serious. And I want you to deliver the check."

When I paid the money on the other couple's tuition, happiness flooded my soul and every trace of bitterness evaporated. I cried rivers of gratitude to God for the wisdom he had given my husband.

March 1989, Loveland, Ohio

I sat on the edge of the tub and gripped the pregnancy test. A single red line mocked my infertility. Over nine months of marriage, but I hadn't become pregnant. I blinked back the tears.

While dating, Gareth and I had discussed our mutual desire for several children. We both grew up in large families and knew the value of sibling friendships. Support from our family and friends had carried us through many of life's tough times. To us, our siblings were an irreplaceable gift from God. We wanted our children to have that same sense of belonging and support.

Even as a young child, I cherished the dream of one day being a mother. I hauled my baby dolls everywhere. Childhood nursery rhymes and romance movies had taught me love, marriage, and family happened naturally, in sequence, and without fail.

To my dismay, pregnancy eluded me. Torturous baby showers cluttered my calendar. Well-meaning friends jokingly assumed my husband and me purposefully delayed having a family. Month after painful month, negative pregnancy results held me on an emotional rollercoaster.

"Dear God, please bless me with children. And give me the grace to trust Your timing."

August 1989

After over a year of trying to conceive, I sought counsel from my pastor's wife. Sitting at her kitchen table, I drew a breath and held it. "Umm … well, every time my husband and I are intimate, I end up having nightmares."

The pastor's wife sipped her coffee. "Hmmm. Were you molested as a child?"

Her question surprised me. "Well … yes. But that was years ago. I don't think of it often. I'm not asking for pity."

"Once we become adults, circumstances can trigger memories of events from our past."

"I've prayed about the dreams." I sighed. "But they're still a problem."

"Have you tried reading the Psalms?"

I shook my head.

"Reading the Word of God will cleanse your mind. It's like pouring oil on your soul. Try this. After your time with your husband, read your Bible before turning off the light. Let a Psalm be your final thought as you drift off to sleep."

I followed her instructions and was amazed at the difference. Within a month, my nightmares ceased.

The following spring, we accepted a missionary assignment to China. A month before our scheduled departure, and after several days of low-grade fever and waking up nauseated, I visited my doctor and learned I was expecting. Despite the inconvenient timing, we were thrilled. Travel fatigue, new smells, and strange-tasting food intensified the morning sickness I suffered on our Oriental journeys.

As the child within my womb grew, I wondered if I would be a good mother. Would the generational sins of my family continue with me? Addictions, self-centeredness, moral impurity … I fell to my knees and begged God to cleanse all traces of inherited sin from my soul.

While other mothers seemed to rely on their intuition and discernment, I was enveloped with self-doubt. How would I teach my child godly character qualities when I, myself, was still learning them?

Desperate for help, I hurried to the bookstore and bought dozens of parenting manuals and character-training books. I was determined to learn how to be a good mother.

A few months later, Gareth carried a large box into our apartment. "Did you order something?"

I cringed. "Umm. About that."

"What is it?"

My courage wavered. "A thousand dollars' worth of diet pills."

"Very funny."

I burst into tears.

"You're not kidding?" His jaw tightened.

For the first time, I saw fire flash in my husband's eyes. "A thousand dollars is a *lot* of money—more than two weeks' pay."

I sobbed, recognizing anger in his voice.

His voice trembled with rage. "What do you plan to do with all these pills?"

"Sell them … to my overweight friends. The dealer said … I would double my money."

Gareth rolled his eyes. After a moment of silence, he spoke slowly and with great control. "Promise me you will never again spend over a hundred dollars without *first*, asking me, and *second*, praying about it for twenty-four hours."

I hung my head in shame, knowing I deserved a scolding and expecting worse. His kindness destroyed me. "Aren't you going to yell and say hurtful things?"

Gareth wrapped his arms around me. "I love you." He smoothed my hair. "Life's too short for fighting. Let's just be friends."

A more incredible friend I had never met, and miracle of miracles, I was married to him.

June 1990

On our second anniversary, Gareth asked, "When did you know for sure that you wanted to marry me?"

"Oh, that's easy," I said. "When I received a dozen roses with the card signed, *I love you*."

"Wait ... what roses? What card?"

"You sent me long-stemmed roses when I was in Texas."

"No. Not roses. Daisies."

"What about the message?" I asked.

"My brother—." Gareth paused and smiled.

I kissed him smack-dab on the lips. "No going back now, bro."

December 1990

After two and a half years of marriage, I gave birth to a healthy baby boy named Gary.

I cried out to God for discernment and guidance every day. I began with this simple prayer: "Dear loving Heavenly Father, thank You for sending Gary to our house. Thank You for trusting us with the responsibility of raising him to be a servant of the King."

In time, after the nightly bedtime story, he bowed his head while I prayed. "Father, thank You for your help today. Give Gary good thoughts and dreams. Please give us the wisdom we need to honor You tomorrow."

I tucked in his sheets and leaned in to kiss his forehead. "Time to sleep. Rest your brain, sweetie. Tomorrow's gonna be a good day."

Each day, my husband rose and left for work while Gary and me still slept. And each evening, Gareth returned in time for dinner. My child's father spent his evenings and weekends making memories with our son, setting an example of a godly father, and being present in his life.

I thanked God every day for these blessings.

April 1994

Three-year-old Gary pulled at my skirt with serious urgency. "Mum, are you and Dad married?"

"Yes."

"When are you going to have another baby?"

"Babies aren't sold at Walmart. Be patient."

But my patience with trying to conceive again had run thin. I confided my infertility to close friends and requested their prayers. Neither advice from my doctor, nor that from friends, worked. I spent hours reading nutrition books and exploring natural remedies.

I searched the Scriptures for a promise and shared with relatives my hope that God would give us a little girl. I purchased a decorative pillow embossed with the name "Joy" and displayed it on my couch.

But every new moon, my emotions crashed with the return of my monthly cycle.

Then I wondered about adoption. What about all those foster children waiting, longing for a family? A fresh wave of gratitude for my adoptive parents washed over me. I had lived as a beggar, a forlorn child. I knew the desperation that came with facing an unknown future, alone. Indeed, I would be the perfect adoptive mother. I could relate to a foster child's need to belong and be loved.

So, I asked Gareth, "Are you open to adopting?"

"I'm willing to consider it."

I called the adoption agencies and filled out the paperwork. I marked foster training dates on the calendar. But when the time came to sign the forms, Gareth hesitated.

"What's wrong, dear?" I asked.

"I'm just not sure about adopting. I doubt I could ever love a stranger as much as I love our son, my flesh and blood. It wouldn't be fair to the other child."

"I appreciate your honesty." I swallowed hard and prayed for wisdom. "But parental love is a gift from God. He multiplies that love with each child you receive, biological or adopted."

Gareth hung his head. "Sorry. I can't do it."

I let it go, until a few months later. A friend called

saying her teenage daughter had recently given birth to a little girl. My friend discovered her granddaughter lying in a basket beneath a tree at the local park, abandoned. Child Protective Services wanted to grant her guardianship of the baby, but she feared that would further alienate her daughter, the baby's mother.

"So why are you calling me?" I asked.

"I want you to adopt my grandbaby."

And there it was. The golden opportunity I'd been waiting for, but Gareth's earlier hesitation dampened my excitement.

"I'll have to talk with my husband," I said. "We'll get back with you."

Gareth's enthusiasm surprised me. "I know you've dreamed of having a daughter. Let's pray about this for a couple of days before we decide."

That night, I arose in the quiet darkness and settled on the couch. I recalled a recent gathering where I had overheard a conversation—a woman shared that she and her husband had sent a letter to this specific pregnant teenager. In that letter, they related their heartbreak of infertility and expressed their desire for a child. They told the teen they would willingly adopt her baby if she found motherhood too overwhelming or needed a way out.

I had to admit, I empathized with the barren woman.

"This is God answering your prayer for a daughter," Gareth said the next day.

"Maybe. But I also prayed that if this child were meant to be ours, no one else would claim her. I know another couple reached out to the expectant mother, first. We should step back and let them have her."

Gareth squeezed my hand. A sense of peace settled in my soul, and I knew we had made the right decision.

Another tick of the clock, and my childbearing window closed. But I knew God was faithful. I hoped one day to gain a daughter when my son married, a precious daughter-in-law, who would be the mother to my future grandbabies.

CHAPTER TWENTY-FOUR

Shocked

December 1996, Toronto, Ontario
Susan

With wet snow sliding down the windshield of our pickup, we drove a desolate stretch of slippery freeway in Buffalo, New York. Marcus and his wife, Stacey, were preparing a joint birthday party for our sons, born one week apart. We pushed through the messy weather and arrived on time.

After the party, Stacey and I dressed our boys in their snowsuits and sent them outside.

"Frightful cold out there," my birth Mum said.

"Will you join us for tea?" Stacey asked.

Mum folded her arms and leaned against the door frame. "Oh, think I'll stand here for a bit and watch the kids."

Stacey set the table with porcelain teacups and plenty of cream and sugar, while I arranged freshly baked snickerdoodles on a plate.

Mum entered the dining room, frowning. "The kids left the yard. I can't see them."

"Don't worry, Mum," Marcus said. "They probably

went to the playground."

"But, you shouldn't let them wander off. It's dangerous, right?"

I lifted the whistling kettle to pour hot water into our cups.

"When we were youngsters, we played in the subways all over Toronto, day and night." Gentleness laced my brother's tone. "No one watched out for us, eh?"

I remembered how we waited for a lull in the human traffic at the train stations, then slid down the escalator handrails.

"What? I never let you kids out of my sight," Mum said in a rush.

Excuse me? I paused the kettle mid-air and shot a glance at my brother.

Marcus averted his gaze.

Mum retreated to the front door.

Stacey filled the cookie sheet with a fresh batch of snickerdoodles and placed them in the oven. The sweet aroma of cinnamon filled the room.

Marcus drummed his fingers on the table. "The adoption crushed Mum and Dad. After you left, Dad binged on liquor and wound up in a homeless shelter."

I sat across from him. "Yes, I know about that."

"The guilt of abandoning you destroyed Mum and pushed her to the brink of insanity," Marcus said without emotion. "She admitted herself to a psychiatric ward where the doctors shocked her brain, right?"

My brother gave me a blank stare that held neither blame for my choice to go to America, nor sympathy for the pain this new information brought me. I blinked back tears, trying to mirror his neutral expression.

"The treatments scrambled her memory, but the guilt

remains," Marcus said. "I see it in her eyes and hear it in her voice, eh? A sense of regret blurs each moment of every day."

The realization of the depth of my mother's suffering sent waves of compassion and sadness rippling through me. I tightened my grip on the teacup. "I once heard a preacher say that God made man to live in harmony with his Creator. He said our bodies and emotions are not designed to carry the debilitating weight of guilt."

Marcus raised his eyebrow. "I guess."

The front door slammed, and Mum ushered the children into the hallway. "I found them." She removed their boots and mittens, then refilled the teapot I'd abandoned. "Why such long faces? A fresh cup of tea will lighten your mood, eh?"

Marcus faked a chuckle.

"Can I fix you another cup of tea, dear?" Mum asked.

"Only if you'll join me." I forced a smile. *My poor Mum.*

"Ohhh, you know, I'm always ready for a cup of tea. How about you, Marcus?"

"I'm good, thanks."

Mum sat opposite me and poured a tablespoon of tea onto her plate.

"What's with pouring tea into your saucer?" I pressed the warm teacup against my lips.

"I guess I don't rightly know, Suzie-Q. I'm copying Nan. Habit, I suppose." She giggled, like Nan.

"Mum?" I drew a quick breath. "We have a lot of catching up to do, like twenty years' worth. Next time you're in Ohio, why not swing by Cincinnati? We'll go out for coffee."

"Hmm ..." Mum gave a slight nod.

The following day, Gareth and I arose at 5 a.m. and packed our bags.

I heard Marcus ascend the stairs. "Susan, Mum's here with her luggage. She says she's going home with you."

"You can't be serious."

"She said she's been waiting for an invitation, and yesterday you gave her one."

Gulp. A thousand questions ran through my mind. How long would she stay? How would she get back home? Where would she sleep?

"Our truck only seats three," I said. "It's too cold for anyone to ride in the back." I faced my husband. "Oh, Gareth, we can't tell her *no*. She'll never speak to me again. What should we do?"

"Hmmm ..." Gareth stroked his chin. "I'll slip out the back door, take the Greyhound, and meet you in Cincinnati."

I should have known he would quickly figure out a way.

I drove the Nissan back to Ohio, dropped my mother and son at our apartment, and pulled into the Greyhound station a few moments after ten. But Gareth's bus hadn't arrived. Having taken the bus from Cincinnati to Toronto on several occasions, I knew their schedule served as merely a suggestion. But two hours late? What could have happened?

Finally, after midnight, Gareth's bus arrived. I learned his lack of luggage set the immigration officials on high alert and cost him an interrogation session. When Gareth explained he yielded his seat to his mother-in-law, the guards rolled their eyes and smirked. Gareth's unbelievable story heightened their suspicion that he was hiding information from them.

After a long delay and lacking hard evidence of a

crime, they finally released him to continue his journey. I was just glad to have him home.

For the entire month of her visit, every morning I awoke to find Mum sitting on the rocking chair, her feet tucked up under her. And every evening, my husband and I fell asleep to a rhythmic squeak of the rocker as Mum sat alone in the dark, late into the night.

She tried to hide the sadness enveloping her. But I noticed her lack of energy and enthusiasm for minimal tasks. Could she be suffering from depression or were these residual side effects of the shock treatments?

"Mum, let's go shopping," I said one day.

"No, I'm comfortable here, Do-Bee."

I waved three tickets in the air. "Children's theater, *Peter Rabbit*. Care to join us?"

"No, you run along. I'll be here when you get back," Mum said.

On the way home from the theater, I purchased a cross-stitch project. If Mum insisted on remaining glued to the rocker, I would settle on the couch and sew.

Later that evening, Mum rocked and listened as I recounted stories about our life in Kansas. She had missed so much, not only in my life but also in the lives of my siblings.

"Do you want to ask me anything?" I offered.

"No."

"Any particular stories you'd like to hear?"

"No."

"Chocolates?" I moved the candy dish toward her.

She laughed. "I'm always ready for sweets."

"Would you like a quiet time?"

"No. I enjoy hearing your voice." Mum smiled softly.

"I can tell you a Bible story," I said.

She nodded, giving me permission.

"Do you have a Bible?"

"A worker at a halfway house gave me one. But I never read it."

"I have an extra. We can study together."

"Um … no. Like I told the hostel worker, I'm not a religious person." She closed her eyes and rocked back in her chair.

The desire to share my faith in Christ with my mother burned within me. If only Mum would yield her life to Jesus. My disappointment must have shown.

"Now, Suzie-Q." Mum winked. "Cheer up. Like I told my friend at the hostel, I'll make my peace with God when I'm ready."

Despite her lack of enthusiasm for spiritual topics, Mum stood first in line at the car and accompanied us to three church services a week.

Toward the end of her visit, Marcus called. "I heard you dragged Mum to church."

"And?"

"She said the people stand, wave their arms above their heads, and shout 'Praise God!' She said for each service they use dozens of Kleenex. And she thinks everyone in your church is on the verge of a nervous breakdown."

I chuckled.

"I'll drive down to get Mum the end of next week," Marcus said.

During Mum's visit, we banked priceless memories, and I treasured every moment.

Several times, Mum shared cooking tips. "You don't

need to kill that potato; it's already dead. And taste the soup before adding more salt."

My joy multiplied every time Mum played with my son, Gary, or held lengthy conversations with my husband. But in my interactions with my mother, the deeper issues of the heart remained untapped.

Once, my frustration got the better of me. "Why did you come here if you won't talk to me?"

Tears shone in her eyes. "I wanted a window into your life."

I understood. My siblings and I sent letters and phone calls back and forth across the miles. But nothing gave me a clearer picture of their lives like spending a few days in their homes.

Susan Carter

CHAPTER TWENTY-FIVE

Make My Day

February 1998, Loveland, Ohio
Susan

We'd enjoyed our usual, beautiful Sunday. We spent the morning in church, had friends over for dinner, and took an afternoon nap. That evening as we prepared for bed, the phone rang.

"Gareth, it's probably your mother," I said.

"Sweetheart, it's for you," Gareth called a moment later.

I entered the living room and picked up the receiver. "Hello?"

"Uh … yeah. Hi," a lady said.

Polly? What's wrong with her voice?

"This is Rose. Your sister."

What? Hadn't I once heard Mum mention Rose? At the time, I hadn't taken her seriously. If I had a mystery sister, my relatives would have told me. Right? Or maybe not.

"Hello, Rose."

"I just learned about you today." Her voice quivered

with nervousness.

"And I'm learning about you right now," I said.

We shared a laugh. I was talking with a total stranger who claimed to be my sister. *Bizarre.* How could I be sure she wasn't mistaken?

"How did you find out about me?"

"This afternoon, my husband and I had dinner with Marcus, and he mentioned his sister, Susan. I asked him about you."

My family was already complicated. Bringing another sister to the mix simply added a new dimension. "Please start at the beginning. How did you find Marcus?"

"I was adopted as a baby." Rose coughed. "You knew about me, right?"

"Well, I heard whispers."

"When I turned forty, I realized I had no clue who I was. Like, who were my parents? What nationality am I? Do I have siblings? So, I called the adoption agency. First, I asked about the process of meeting my birth mother. They communicated with Madeline and secured permission to release her contact information to me. Once they gave me Madeline's—uh, Mum's phone number—I called and set a time and place to meet her."

"It's alright to call her Madeline. After all, she's still a stranger to you, right?"

"Yeah, thanks. So, we had dinner."

"Awkward for both of you, I'm sure."

Rose giggled, still clearly nervous. "We met at a restaurant in Toronto. I learned my birth was the result of a one-night stand. That kind of hurt, eh?"

"I can imagine. I'm sorry."

"I asked Madeline if I had any siblings, and she told me about Marcus. I couldn't stop crying. They were tears of happiness, right? I was so happy to discover I had a biological brother. I have an adopted brother, but we're not close."

"I'm sorry to hear that. My brothers and sisters are my best friends."

"Whoa! Did you say brothers *and* sisters? As in more than one? Wow! Knowing I'm not alone in the world completes my happiness. How many siblings do I have?"

"Counting Marcus and me, you have four sisters and four brothers."

"What a discovery! I look forward to meeting everyone."

I learned she'd had a fairly happy life. Rose's adoptive parents had immigrated to Canada from Ukraine. She'd grown up attending Ukrainian summer camps, eating Ukrainian food, and learning the language. She'd known she was loved.

"Marcus showed me your picture," Rose said. "I'd like to meet you. Could you come up to Toronto say, next week?"

"Sure, I can."

Toronto was definitely not a half-way point, but I didn't mind driving the distance. Besides, she no doubt had a day job and couldn't take the time off, while my schedule as a stay-at-home mom was more flexible. After all, she was family, right? And I was beyond excited to meet her.

Four days later, Gary and I found ourselves waiting inside an A&W restaurant in the suburbs of Toronto.

"I can't wait to meet Aunt Rose." Gary sipped his root

beer. "How will you know if she's your sister?"

"I'll know." A nervous tension tightened in the pit of my stomach.

Moments later, Gary tapped my arm. "Mum, Aunt Rose pulled into the parking lot."

"Are you sure?"

"She looks like Aunt Polly." He grinned.

As Rose entered the restaurant, we stood to greet her. She'd pulled her hair up into a tight bun on top of her head and a wisp of curls framed her face, the same style Polly often wore. Rose stopped before me and offered a handshake, but I pulled her in for a hug.

"Oh, okay." She returned my embrace. "I live close to here. I have lunch ready. Do you have time to come over?"

"Of course."

We followed Rose through a maze of subdivisions to her beautiful new home. Ivan, her Ukrainian husband, met us at the door. The delicious aroma of a home-cooked meal greeted us as we entered. She escorted us through the living room and straight to the elegant dining room table, where she served cabbage rolls, roasted carrots, and homemade bread.

I folded my hands. "Do you mind if I offer a prayer of thanks for the food?"

Ivan stiffened.

"What did the cabbage say at the salad bar?" Rose asked.

I had no idea what to make of her question.

"Lettuce pray," she said.

Everyone laughed. Ivan relaxed, and we bowed our heads while I prayed.

I bit into a cabbage roll. "The food is delicious."

"Yeah, Ukrainian meals are my favorite," Rose said.

"Ivan says I'm a better cook than his mother."

"Aunt Rose," Gary said, "please give my Mum this recipe."

Rose beamed, then glanced at me. "You have a lazy eye and a lisp, like me."

"I do."

"And we're both prematurely gray."

"During my college days I dyed my hair."

"What made you quit?'

"A batch of bad dye turned my hair green the night before we left on a vacation to see my husband's family," I said. "I decided I'd rather be naturally gray than humiliatingly green."

Rose threw back her head and laughed.

I finished the last bite of caramel apple dumpling and set my fork on the dessert plate. "Do you have any children?"

Their tri-level home featured several bedrooms and a finished basement. They also had a fenced-in yard, perfect for a puppy. Since it was lunchtime on a weekday, I assumed their kids were in school.

"No. No children." Rose giggled. "We wrote a detailed prenuptial contract. No children, no pets."

Obviously, the predisposition to chuckle when nervous ran through her genes as it did the other women in my family.

Ivan lifted his chin. "We are godparents to my niece in Ukraine."

Godparents? Our cultural differences became increasingly clear with each passing moment. I sensed an awkward tension building.

Rose grimaced at her husband and tapped her teacup.

"Everything alright?" I asked.

She stood. "I'm sorry, but I'm going to have to ask you to leave."

I flopped back in my chair, openly displaying my surprise.

She leaned close. "It's my neighbors, right?" She lowered her voice. "They're friends with my adopted father. If your car is here too long, they'll want to know who came to visit, and I don't want them to know about you, eh?"

Her expression insinuated I should understand. I didn't.

"But I haven't shown you any pictures of our siblings."

Rose glanced at Ivan. "I guess we can take a peek at your photos."

Gary jumped from his chair. "I'll help clear the table." He carried plates to the kitchen.

Rose led me into the living room. Elegant wooden furniture and ornate lamps flanked a beautiful stone fireplace. An almond-scented candle burned on the mantel beside a lovely bouquet of silk flowers. I made a mental note to send her something with flowers for Christmas.

We sat in wing-backed chairs where the light from the bay window streamed over our shoulders. I pulled photos from my purse. "This is our brother, Davie."

"Ah, we share the same brown eyes," she said.

"And this is Polly."

Rose carefully studied the picture. "There's a strong resemblance here. You can tell we're sisters. Well, technically half-sisters."

"We're family." I held up the last photo. "This is Aulden and Thomas."

"Aulden resembles Marcus."

"I agree," I said.

Rose closed the album. "We'll walk you to your car."

Outside, I opened the car door and threw in my jacket. "You're welcome to come to visit. The town to the south of us has a flower show every April. We can start making memories."

Her dark eyes sparkled. "You're on. I have a passion for flowers."

"We'll plan on it."

Ivan hovered at Rose's side, and once again I sensed that awkward tension.

"No, that won't work," Rose said.

"Why?"

Rose licked her lips. "If we're gone for more than a day, my father will wonder where we went. He'll start asking questions, right? If I tell him the truth, he'll write me out of his will, eh? And, well, we need the money to pay for this house."

The neighbor's garage door hummed as it rose. With a silent wave good-bye, Ivan went back inside.

"We can at least exchange Christmas and birthday cards, right?" I asked. I hoped I hadn't come this far only to have these few moments with her.

"My father reads all my cards. If he sees a name he doesn't recognize, he'll ask about you."

"I'll call you sometime." My last-ditch effort.

Rose shook her head. "My dad's here a lot. He might answer the phone."

Had Rose searched for her birth family simply to affirm her own identity? I could only imagine the confusion of knowing nothing about one's own history. And Rose had just turned forty. She was right on target for a mid-life crisis.

The air smelled of coming rain. I snapped my fingers, motioning for Gary to get in the car.

"So, it's goodbye." I kissed my sister's cheek and got behind the wheel.

"Thanks for coming," she said. "You made my day."

I drove away, turning west on the 401 freeway and headed back to Cincinnati as thunder rumbled and lightning flashed.

Gary turned down the music and glanced my way. "Are you sad, Mum?"

I blew out a long, slow breath. "It's not enough to share a bloodline and have similar mannerisms, right? You can be family, and at the same time, be strangers."

Raindrops pelted the windshield and drummed on the hood. I turned on the wipers.

"Relationships are built over time." I slapped the steering wheel for emphasis. "Sharing life, being there for each other in the good times and through the difficult times."

I could tell Gary was trying to understand, so I went on.

"I had hoped to add another sister to my family." I struggled to swallow back tears. "Instead, I met a woman who is either unwilling or unable to invest her time or energy to make this relationship a reality. In four days, I've gained and lost a sister. Tough week."

CHAPTER TWENTY-SIX

The Calling

March 1999, Loveland, Ohio
Susan

Gareth sat on the couch with his Bible open on his lap. "Susan." His eyes twinkled. "It's time to go."

"Where are we going?"

"To the mission field."

Whoa! I needed a moment to process. Gareth loved his job as a master electrician. In the evenings, he pored over electrical magazines, and on the weekends, he hung out at the local hardware store. This would be a total life change for us.

But did he mean right then, that month, or next year? Or in five years?

Would we sell our house or rent it out? How often would we come back to visit? Or were we too old to learn a new language?

During our college days, Gareth had served as the president of the missionary prayer group. His love for people and his interest in reaching the lost were qualities I'd always admired.

I had assumed we would go to the mission field right after Gareth's graduation. But paying bills took priority. Then the baby came, and for twenty years life happened. Yet, every time our church called for volunteers for a mission trip, we went. We'd been to Asia, South and Central America, and Europe.

We'd talked of this dream so many times. But this time, I sensed Gareth meant it.

I retreated to my room and prayed. "Lord, are You in this decision? Are You asking me to leave my town, my home, and my family?"

Remember the cyst?

My thoughts raced back to when I was a teenager and knelt at an altar during our summer camp meeting. I wrestled with the idea of preparing to be a missionary. I wondered if the desire were a passing dream or an appointment from God.

All that summer, I had nursed a hideous cyst on my eyelid. Daily, I smothered the bump with olive oil that ran down my cheeks and blurred my vision.

That night at the altar, I buried my head in the crook of my arm and cried out to God. "If You want me to be a missionary, will You heal my eye?"

By the next day, the redness of the cyst had begun fading, and it had shrunk. Within a month, the bump disappeared. That was over thirty years before.

I returned to the living room and found my husband. "What's our first step?"

Soon, we completed an application for the position of full-time missionaries. We traveled to churches to raise financial support.

Then, during a trip to southwest Florida, my cousin contacted me concerning my birth mother's health. "Susan, your mother has an inoperable brain aneurysm. You'd better come to visit her."

Gareth and I immediately traveled north to my mother's home in a village on the shores of Lake Huron. When we arrived, I was anxious to deal with spiritual issues. But would Mum listen? She had put me off twice before.

I sat on her couch, that was covered in cat hair, and leaned forward. "Mum, we know you are dying. You know you're dying. It's time to make your peace with God. May we read the Bible and pray with you?"

Silence reigned while Mum contemplated.

Tears flowed down my cheeks. I pressed a hand on my quivering gut. *Heavenly Father, no one can come to You without the help of the Holy Spirit. Please gift my mum faith to believe You will forgive her and the courage to forgive herself.*

Finally, Mum nodded. "Yes, dear. That would be fine."

Gareth read Psalm twenty-three.

"Jesus shed His blood on the cross at Calvary to pay for our sins," I said.

Mum sucked in a breath and turned her face to the wall. "I've already suffered for my sins."

"Yes, and I'm sorry for your pain. But only the suffering of Jesus can save your soul. The only way to Heaven is to accept Him as your Savior."

"God loves you and wants to save you," Gareth said.

I scooted to the edge of my seat. "All of your children are serving Jesus. We've missed being a family here on earth, but all of eternity awaits us. God wants you to join Him in Heaven. Wouldn't you like to pray and invite Jesus into your heart?"

"Yes, but I don't know what to say."

I was so overcome with tears of joy, I couldn't speak.

So, I motioned to Gareth.

He led Mum in a simple prayer: "Thank You, Jesus, for dying on the cross for me. God, I pray You would forgive me of my sins. Here I am, Lord. Fill me with your Spirit. In Jesus' name. Amen."

Later that night, doubts plagued my dreams. When Mum had prayed, I didn't see the usual evidence of a changed heart. Her face had shown no change in emotion. She hadn't shed tears of joy or offered praise and thanks to God. I had to know if my mother experienced a genuine conversion.

The following day, we sat together, cradling our coffee mugs. "Mum, when you prayed last night, what was in your mind and heart? Did you pray with sincerity or were you merely trying to make me feel better?"

Mum pursed her lips and shook her head. "If I hadn't meant it, I wouldn't have said it."

Outside, I barely smiled. But inside I was shouting. *Glory to God!*

CHAPTER TWENTY-SEVEN

Reunion

August 2000
Susan

Gareth and I sped west on the interstate toward Missouri. Thomas was getting married and had invited everyone, including our birth parents, to attend. For the past week, I'd been too anxious to eat or sleep. How would my siblings handle this emotionally charged event? I didn't know, but I was praying.

"Why don't you recline your seat and try to get some sleep?" Gareth gently squeezed my hand.

But I knew I couldn't. My mind simply refused to rest.

"I'll give you the camera," I said. "Please take pictures of everything, even if it seems insignificant." I brushed away a tear. "I've lived for this day, dreamt of it, and imagined every detail a thousand times. I don't want to miss a thing."

Dave

He flew two thousand miles from Halifax, Nova Scotia, to Missouri, then spent the night where his son planned to be married. Thomas and his bride had planned their wedding to be a private ceremony in the living room of the bride's home.

This morning, the morning of Thomas' wedding day, Dave woke early and went down the gravel country road for a long walk. As he walked, excitement and nervousness surged through him. More than twenty years ago, he'd left young Polly and the younger boys with their older siblings and skipped town with his wife, Madeline. Today he would reconnect with his children.

Dave's hands shook. He sincerely hoped the memory of his leaving wasn't haunting anyone else and ruining the specialness of the day.

Ever since he'd given up drinking, he had faithfully attended Alcoholics Anonymous. He'd learned the essential steps to finding healing and forgiveness included confessing one's sins to God and apologizing to those one had hurt. This family reunion provided the perfect setting for accomplishing that goal. He purposed to find a private moment with each of his children and extend a heartfelt apology for the grief he had caused them.

A half-hour before the wedding, Dave was again outside, patrolling the yard. He eagerly watched the road, ready to greet everyone as they arrived.

A Chrysler pulled into the drive. Dave's heartbeat quickened. As the driver raised the sun visor, a younger version of himself smiled. Dave struggled to choke back the tears. Davie jumped out, made a beeline for Dave, and placed his son, Davie, Jr., into his grandpa's arms.

Dave thanked God. He never dared to imagine a forgiving reception. He held his grandson to his chest, his heart beating with joy.

Madeline

Madeline hid in the house as cars carrying her children continued to pull into the drive. With a trembling hand, she brushed aside the lace curtain and watched Dave's reunion unfold.

Her intense desire to see her children had outweighed any anxiety over how she would be received, so she'd accepted the invitation and traveled to Missouri. She needed to know her children were well and happy. She needed to know she'd made the right decision in not attending the custody hearing all those years ago.

Madeline didn't expect to be the center of attention, nor did she anticipate kind words from her children. She knew she'd committed an unforgivable sin by abandoning her babies when they needed her the most.

Susan

Gareth and I arrived at the same time my adoptive parents pulled into the yard. I got out of the car and hugged my adoptive father. Arm in arm, we walked toward Dave.

"Father," I said, "I'd like to introduce you to my birth

father, Dave."

Marcus, Davie, Thomas, Polly, and I encircled the two men as they exchanged warm smiles and handshakes.

"I'm so happy to meet you!" Father said.

"The pleasure is all mine, sir," Dave said. "I can never thank you enough for all you've done for my kids."

Polly pulled our adoptive Mother into the circle.

"Our son, Davie, resembles you," Mother said.

Dave beamed. "I hope my kids haven't given you any trouble."

"Oh, we've experienced our share of shenanigans," Mother said.

Everyone laughed.

Our lighthearted group moved inside, ready to enjoy the wedding. The only guests were immediate family members.

After the simple ceremony, we all posed for family pictures. The bride and groom stood front and center, and Mother and Father stepped in beside Thomas. Dave took the spot next to the bride. Madeline joined Marcus and his family at the far right.

Just as the photographer was about to capture his last shot, Aulden and his family arrived. They squeezed in beside Gareth and me.

"You're late," I whispered.

"Car trouble."

"Madeline and Dave are here."

"Means nothin' to me," Aulden said.

I didn't respond, but I was still praying.

Madeline

After the pictures were taken, Madeline approached Polly. "Care to take a walk?"

"Sure," Polly said.

They strolled along the gravel road, past a church, and toward a one-lane bridge. Madeline gauged her daughter's silence and figured neither of them was sure how to start the conversation.

But the worry, the shame, had built in Madeline for too many years. She couldn't wait any longer to say what was in her heart.

She stopped walking. "My baby, my baby! I'm *so* sorry for leaving you."

Polly turned and hugged her. Madeline wrapped her arms around Polly and wept so hard she soaked her daughter's shoulder. Eventually, Madeline stopped trembling.

Polly pulled back and offered a gentle smile. "There's no need to explain. I had a teen pregnancy and gave up my baby for adoption. I understand your remorse, and I forgive you. I hope someday my birth son will find me, because now I'm the one seeking forgiveness."

Madeline almost couldn't believe the grace she'd been offered. "Thank you."

Hand in hand, they walked across the bridge.

Susan

The hum of low conversation filtered through the reception hall as the last of the wedding guests prepared to leave. I took another bite of wedding cake as Marcus approached.

"It hurts to see Mum stand in the corner all day. She wanted to speak to her kids. But she's fearful of rejection," Marcus said.

"I've been watching. Everyone has spoken with her."

Marcus placed his arm on my shoulder and squeezed. "This is a pivotal day for Mum and Dad. They so desperately need resolution and healing."

I brushed a happy tear. "It's changed us all."

And I was so grateful to God—for knowing me and loving me. For providing for me and my siblings even through the pain of abandonment and adoption. Now, He was restoring each individual in my family as He'd done for me. *Hallelujah!*

EPILOGUE

May 2005, Dartmouth, Nova Scotia
Susan

The old stone church echoed as I lifted the strands of "Great Is Thy Faithfulness" at my father's funeral. Almost 200 people had come, including many of my father's Alcoholics Anonymous friends. That he'd touched so many and mattered to so many comforted my heart.

After the funeral, Marcus placed a small metal object in my hand. "Dad would want you to have this."

In my open palm lay my father's Alcoholics Anonymous pin. "Oh my." Tears welled in my eyes. "Twelve years of sobriety. That's fantastic."

"Oh, that was only the halfway point," Marcus said. He opened his fist to reveal Dad's twenty-four-year pin. "You knew Dad was a featured speaker for AA in the Maritime Provinces, right?"

"He told me." I drew Marcus in for a tight embrace. "Yes, I couldn't be prouder."

At the cemetery, I stood with a tight circle of relatives around my father's grave. We overlapped our umbrellas, but a steady drizzle still soaked our backs.

Dad had mentioned his desire for his ashes to be buried in my grandfather's grave. I remembered the hatred

Dad nursed toward his father and marveled at this gesture of forgiveness.

A commotion sounded behind us, and I turned from the interment to see what was happening. A busload of tourists crunched on the gravel path, heading toward the Titanic memorial tombstones thirty feet up the hillside. Aunt Sharon linked my arm and drew me under her black umbrella. The Salvation Army General read the twenty-third Psalm, then led us in the hymn "Amazing Grace."

Later that night, my sister Claire phoned. "Yeah, hi. Sorry I missed the graveside service. I got stuck in traffic, and by the time I arrived at the cemetery you were pulling out. And then I lost you in traffic, again. I didn't follow you to the dinner, because I had no idea where you were going."

"Sorry we missed you."

"That's okay. I do want to spend time with you. May I drive you to the airport tomorrow?"

"I have an early flight and have to check-in three hours prior. I'll totally understand if you change your mind."

"Oh, no, please, I want to do this."

Claire picked me up as promised, and I made my check-in time. Then, we sat in an airport coffee shop and chatted.

"Did you know you had twin sisters?" Claire asked.

"Yes, I did. When you were three, we made dandelion pies together when I visited Grandma. Do you remember that?" I couldn't help noticing how much Claire resembled our father, her blue eyes and thick dark hair.

"No. I wish I did." Claire sipped her coffee.

"I remember it very well," I said, "That was the day I told you and Coleen we were sisters."

"Oh, you did? And what did we say?"

"It must have scared you, because you both cried and ran into the house. Grandma and your mum came out and gave me a good tongue lashing."

"We lived directly above Grandma, right?" Claire's eyes glistened. "Her house was like my second home. We were quite close."

"I thought so," I said. "Grandma once sent a thank-you letter to my adoptive parents. She included your high school graduation picture. And one of Coleen."

Claire looked relieved. "Ah. I wondered how you recognized me at the funeral."

"Where is your sister Coleen? What does she do?"

"She's an interior designer and lives in Quebec. I see her on holidays."

"And do you work outside your home?"

"Why, yes, I'm a paralegal. I help lawyers with their paperwork."

I raised an eyebrow. "Sounds complicated."

"Did Grandma ever say anything to you about me?"

"Only that you were the joy of her life."

Claire smiled, visibly pleased.

I coughed. "Were you close to our father, Dave?"

Claire grimaced. "No. Umm, no, I wasn't."

"Then, why were you at his funeral?"

We locked eyes. "I came to meet you."

"That's lovely." And how wonderful of God to make sure I knew that.

"My adopted dad died of liver cancer." Claire's eyes pooled with tears. "A year later, my mother—your Aunt Letty—died of throat cancer."

The raw pain in her voice made me want to squirm.

Claire cleared her throat. "Coleen and I were fifteen, and our older brother twenty. The court permitted him to raise us. We contacted Dave and asked for financial help. You know, like child support. But, to our amazement, he only cared about himself. We later learned that he wasted all his money on alcohol. I couldn't believe he had no sympathy or sense of responsibility for his own flesh and blood."

I understood her feelings. Hadn't I thought the same?

She paused, drawing in a long breath. "My older brother struggled. It took a lot of hard work and creativity just to survive. I lost respect for Dave after that, never spoke to him again."

"The sweetest revenge—"

Claire nodded, obviously thinking I would agree with her tactics.

"… is forgiveness," I continued.

She seemed confused, as if I hadn't paid attention to her story or felt her pain. "Forgive him? Are you crazy?" She choked at the absurdity of such an idea. "I will *never* forgive him."

I let it drop.

I glanced at my watch and rose. "Time to head for my gate. Call me sometime. Keep in touch."

"Yes, I would like that very much."

I joined the lineup at the security checkpoint. Claire continued walking beside me on the other side of the rope.

"Why don't you come and visit me in Ohio next summer?" I asked. "Our family reunion is in June, and I could introduce you to the rest of your siblings."

Claire pinched her neck. "I'd be too nervous coming by myself." A shy grin played around her lips. "What if I bring Coleen?"

"Of course." I returned her smile.

I placed my belongings in the plastic container and sent them through the x-ray machine. Claire watched in silence. As the security guard motioned me through the scanner, I locked eyes with her, threw her one last hug, and blew a kiss.

Tears glistened in Claire's eyes. She fought them back, smiled bravely, and waved.

"See you later, sweet sister," I whispered. "For us, the story has just begun."

Susan Carter

ACKNOWLEDGMENTS

I laugh when I remember my naivete concerning the writer's journey. I had no idea how involved the process of writing a book would be until I spent hundreds of hours in training, countless hours re-writing drafts, and worked my way through piles and piles of paper and ink. Most of all, I didn't realize writing required a community effort.

Thank you to all my friends and family who courageously read through the poorly written early drafts. Kristal, Deanna, Kiana, Lewis, Lynn, and Kristin. Kristin, it was at your suggestion I included childhood years in Nova Scotia.

Thank you to my friends who painstakingly guided me through the early stages of edits and set my writing on a path to readability and common sense. Daryl Hausman, Shawna Wright, and GraceAnn Moyer.

Thank you to my friends who offered their guidance and suggestions for the discussion questions. Melissa Roe and Valorie Quesenberry.

To the Jerry Jenkins Writer's Guild and the Word Weavers International critique groups in Boone County, KY: Karisa, Kim, Rachel, Pam, Judy, Amy; and Page 34: Templa, Andy, Stephanie, and Lee Ann—thank you. Your input and suggestions were invaluable. You make me want to keep writing; thankfully, I'm one and done.

Thank you, Karen Mills, my dear friend, for your willingness to read and reread draft after painful draft, always with a smile and word of encouragement. I would never have completed this book without you.

To my editor and friend, Shellie Arnold, thank you. I am forever grateful God sent you into my life. Because of your insight and expertise, this work is polished and respectable.

Thanks to the children who modeled for the front cover photo—Rebekah, Mary, Robbie, Hunter, and Wyatt.

Thank you to Kevin Miles Moser who took the photo and designed the cover.

To my beloved husband, Gareth, who patiently sat through hundreds of hours of readings, gave countless words of encouragement, and repeatedly reminded me the result would be worth the effort, thank you. I would not have had the courage to write a book without your support.

And to my Lord and Savior, Jesus Christ, it is because of your grace and mercy that I have a story worth telling. I give You all the glory!

Dear Reader,

I want to share a map of my healing journey.
My journey began when I was twelve and trusted
Jesus as my Lord and Savior. I John 1:9 says, "If we
confess our sins, He is faithful and just to forgive us
our sins and to cleanse us from all unrighteousness." I
cried out to Jesus and asked Him to forgive my sins
and heal my soul.

Over the years, the story of Jesus healing the
crippled man lying beside the pool of Bethesda has
continually stirred my heart. Jesus knew the man had
suffered all his life, and without a divine touch, he
had no hope. In His mercy, Jesus asked the man, "Do
you want to be made well?" (John 5:6).

Like that man, I was crippled by emotional
baggage. Without God's transforming power, my life
pointed toward tragedy. The day I met Jesus, He saw
my brokenness and initiated my healing. I rejoiced in
my newfound faith in Christ and praised God for His
mercy to me. Imagine my joy when I discovered John
1:12. "But as many as received Him, to them He gave
the right to become children of God, to those who
believe in His name." God adopted me into *His*
family!

The Holy Spirit's presence brought assurance
of my salvation and the gift of peace. I *knew* I was a
child of God, a valued daughter of the King, a
princess, as Romans 8:16 explains. "The Spirit Himself
bears witness with our spirit that we *are* children of
God." (emphasis mine) My joy increased when I read
all of Romans 8 and learned nothing can separate me
from God's love. Knowing I am secure in my

heavenly Father's love gave me comfort. He is always there for me. His love is extravagant, boundless, and everlasting.

My adoptive parents gave me a Bible, and I began studying the Word. Ephesians 4:32 really caught my attention. "And be kind to one another, tenderhearted, forgiving one another, even as God in Christ forgave you." I understood that if I accepted God's forgiveness, I must then be willing to forgive others. God has helped me practice forgiveness, whether or not the offender has attempted to reconcile with me.

My Sunday school classmates at that time, who grew up attending church, could recite Scripture passages. They knew of Bible characters like David, Noah, and Elijah, but I didn't. So, I saved my babysitting money, bought a study Bible and a Strong's Concordance, and began the daily discipline of studying God's Word. As my knowledge of Scripture grew, so did my faith, and my confidence in the God I worshiped deepened. A favorite verse from that time is "So then faith *comes* by hearing, and hearing by the word of God." (Romans 10:17).

During my teen years, pouting was my go-to attitude. When things didn't go my way, I'd pout, pout, pout. One day my mother told me life would be more pleasant if I refused to give in to moodiness. Then, I discovered Psalm 16:11, "You will show me the path of life; in Your presence *is* fullness of joy;" and I thought, *If God dwells in my soul, shouldn't my life radiate joy?* As I spent time in God's presence through Bible reading and prayer, my joy increased and my tendency to pout diminished.

After I became an adult, God's Spirit revealed a root of bitterness in my heart caused by buried hurts I had refused to address. He showed me the dark stain of anger in my soul. When I surrendered those hurts to Jesus, a deep peace replaced those hurts.

The Lord used my husband to teach me to avoid bitterness by quickly forgiving others. Together, we studied Matthew 5:44. "But I say to you, love your enemies, bless those who curse you, do good to those who hate you, and pray for those who spitefully use you and persecute you." Now when I am offended, I look for ways to show love to the offender, like praying blessing over their life.

From James 3:11, I learned it's impossible to simultaneously bless (love) and curse (hold a grudge against) another person. "Does a spring send forth fresh *water* and bitter from the same opening?"

As I grew in my relationship with God, my focus broadened to include ministry. Yes, there were times when the trials and complications of life rocked my world, but my faith held. The strong foundation of Biblical principles I had gleaned from the Word of God anchored me amid chaos.

A desire to serve led my husband and me to full-time mission work, which is why I'm a missionary today. From experience, I know work in ministry develops patience. Our American culture delights in quick results, but spiritual harvesting takes time. When I'm tempted to be disheartened with our ministry progress, I remind myself of Galatians 6:9. "And let us not grow weary while doing good, for in due season we shall reap if we do not lose heart."

In 2015, my husband and I attended a missionary training course in Colorado. While there, I learned another valuable lesson—the importance of cultivating a spirit of gratitude. I Thess. 5:18 says, "In everything, give thanks, for this is the will of God in Christ Jesus for you." You have read my life story. You *know* I have a million reasons to be thankful. I'm embarrassed to say I have not always practiced gratitude. But I have *learned* to praise God *on purpose* every day. In turn, He increases my joy. I praise Him for little things like a beautiful sunrise or a call from a friend. And I praise Him for big things like the arrival of a new grandbaby.

Our lives are complicated and our wounds multi-leveled, yet God knows the most effective healing journey for each of us. One of my favorite Scripture passages is Psalm 103:1-4. "Bless the LORD, O my soul, and all that is within me, *bless* His holy name! Bless the LORD, O my soul, and forget not *all* His benefits: Who forgives all your iniquities, Who heals all your diseases, Who redeems your life from destruction, Who crowns you with lovingkindness and tender mercies." (second emphasis mine)

Your journey won't look exactly like mine. But the Scripture tells us that soul healing is part of God's plan for broken humanity. By faith, thank Him in advance for *your* healing.

Lovingly,
Susan

STUDY QUESTIONS

Chapter One: It's Complicated

1. What does God's Word say about brokenness?
   (see Psalm 34:18)
2. Why is loneliness so powerful?
3. How can the influence of a friend guide us into right or
   wrong decisions? (see Proverbs 13:20)

Chapter Two: Happy Valentine's

1. What circumstances or emotions fed Maddie and Dave's
   feelings of broken trust? How is the feeling of regret
   illustrated in this chapter?
2. What is true forgiveness? How should we deal with the
   reminders of past hurts?
3. How do we know every child is planned by God?
   (see Jeremiah 1:5)

Chapter Three: Lazy Days of Summer

1. In what negative ways did Maddie and Dave react to each
   other's faults?
2. How do you usually deal with disappointment?
3. Will God disappoint us? (see Micah 7:7)

Chapter Four: Baby Blues

1. How can our pain keep us from considering another's
   perspective or needs?
2. What symptoms of depression were evident in Madeline's
   life? How can we support someone suffering from

depression?

3. How does the Biblical concept of "burden bearing" apply to believers? (see Galatians 6:2)

Chapter Five: Giggles and Tears

1. In what ways is the theme of abandonment prominent in this chapter? Why is abandonment a serious emotional issue?
2. Will God ever leave us? (see Deut. 31:6)
3. What types of security did the children experience with Nan? What are some examples of the security and constancy we find in God? (see Psalm 91)

Chapter Six: Major Move

1. How did Dave's drinking contribute to instability and loss for his family?
2. How do addictions and unhealthy habits tend to affect our family members?
3. What part do we play in obtaining victory over temptation? (see James 4:7)

Chapter Seven: Burst My Balloon

1. How do we know Susan felt unloved and misunderstood?
2. How was your childhood affected by your family's or a particular family member's lifestyle?
3. What help does God offer those who attempt to overcome addictions? (see I Cor. 10:13)

Chapter Eight: Merry Christmas

1. When has an act of kindness encouraged you?
2. How can your words bring hope and confidence to others? (see Proverbs 25:11)
3. How are we to treat the poor and needy? (see Deut. 15:11)

Chapter Nine: Darkness

1. What kind of adult choices were Susan and her siblings forced to make?
2. As a child, Susan couldn't comprehend God's care for her. When in your life were you unaware of God's presence and aid?
3. Describe the refuge we can find in God. (see Deut. 33:27)

Chapter Ten: The Secret

1. How did Maddie's flirting and Dave's jealous anger toward his wife harm their children?
2. When have you seen your behavior, anger, or jealousy affecting others?
3. What does Scripture say to those who feel lonely or abandoned? (see Deut. 31:6-8)

Chapter Eleven: Emergency Shelter

1. Susan wanted to protect her siblings from the social services lady. When have you felt a fierce sense of protection over someone?
2. How can Christians demonstrate God's love to the needy? Why is this important in our society? (see James 1:27a)
3. How does God's love manifest to those who are

abandoned and forsaken? (see Psalm 27:10)

Chapter Twelve: Foster Care

1. How did Mum Jenkins' investment in Susan help her confidence? When have you gone out of your way to inspire a child?
2. Describe your own desire for a parent's love and the effect of its presence or absence in your life.
3. How did Jesus connect having a childlike heart attitude with receiving salvation? (see Matthew 18:3)

Chapter Thirteen: The Visit

1. How did God use Mum Jenkins to stabilize the lives of Susan and her siblings?
2. What does God say we become when we accept Jesus and become part of His family? (see Romans 8:17)
3. How does being an heir of God's kingdom contrast with the treatment Susan and her siblings received as foster children?

Chapter Fourteen: Family Bonds

1. Describe a time when you felt left out of a social group or weren't included in a way you would like to have been.
2. When have you given God less than your best or a "consolation prize," like the vanity set Susan received from her Mum?
3. How does Scripture say we are to love God? (see Matthew 22:37)

Chapter Fifteen: Released

1. Did you feel sorry for Madeline and Dave when they lost their children? Why, or why not?
2. Have you ever gone out of your way to minister to a homeless person or orphan? Why or why not?
3. When life's uncertainties come at us, how and why should we give our burdens to God? (see I Peter 5:7)

Chapter Sixteen: New Parents

1. Describe a time of great loss and uncertainty in your life.
2. Staying with Mum Jenkins was only temporary provision for Susan and her siblings. When have you experienced temporary provision?
3. What does Scripture say about the changing seasons of our lives? (see Eccl. 3:1-8)

Chapter Seventeen: Roadblock

1. How can the presence of sin hinder maturity in our lives?
2. How did God use Linda as an ambassador of love and care to the children?
3. When has God used you to be an ambassador of love and care to others? Discuss. (see Matthew 10:42)

Chapter Eighteen: Welcome Home

1. How can disappointment in our childhood or a previous relationship potentially hinder our ability to receive affection as adults or in a new relationship?
2. How can that disappointment or wound affect how we see and label ourselves?

3. How did Susan's salvation experience mark the beginning of a new identity? (see II Cor. 5:17). What does Scripture say God will give those who continue in relationship with Christ? (see Rev. 2:17b)

Chapter Nineteen: Growing Pains

1. Valorie's arrival in Susan's new home created new challenges for Susan. When has the unexpected caused stress in your life?
2. Discuss how difficult being open and friendly to others can be when we're hurting.
3. Sometimes we forget those around us have their own stories of hurt and loss. How did reading Grandma Goldie's letter affect Susan? What does Scripture say we all have in common? (see Romans 3:23)

Chapter Twenty: Reconnection and Direction

1. Discuss how difficult forgiving others is while harboring bitterness.
2. How did Susan's path to forgiving her biological parents begin?
3. What encouragement does Scripture give about forgiving others? Discuss. (see Eph. 4:32)

Chapter Twenty-one: Answered Prayer and Heartbreak

1. Dave's letter of confession convinced Susan of his salvation. How does Scripture connect believing on Jesus with confession and salvation? (see Romans 10:9-10)
2. What clues indicated Ken didn't have a deep love for Susan?

3. Describe a time your dreams or plans failed. What does Scripture say about God's plans for us? (see Jeremiah 29:11)

Chapter Twenty-two: Fresh Start

1. During Susan's transition away from Ken, how was God's love demonstrated to her by others?
2. How did God use Susan's work, and her testimony, to bring her and Gareth together?
3. How does Scripture connect delighting ourselves in the Lord with having our desires fulfilled? (see Psalm 37:4-5)

Chapter Twenty-three: New Beginnings

1. What lesson did Susan learn from the dream about her mother and Jesus?
2. What was Gareth's remedy for dissolving bitterness?
3. The pastor's wife counseled Susan to read Scripture to help heal her wound of sexual trauma. Discuss how focusing on God's truth and allowing Him to work within us can bring healing from deep wounds. (see Ephesians 5:26)

Chapter Twenty-four: Shocked

1. How can guilt become a wall between us and others? Between us and God?
2. When have you gone out of your way to demonstrate love for another, as Gareth did for his mother-in-law?
3. What does Scripture say is God's perspective of those who are spiritually lost? (see II Peter 3:9)

Chapter Twenty-five: Make My Day

1. Susan was well into adulthood before God led her to meet her sister, Rose. Describe an instance you waited a long time for God to fulfill a dream.
2. When have you reached out to someone, only to discover they didn't have time for you or didn't want to connect as you had hoped?
3. What does Scripture say about the value of waiting on God? (see Isaiah 40:31)

Chapter Twenty-six: The Calling

1. What confirmations did God give Susan that now was the time for her and Gareth to become missionaries?
2. Why did Susan doubt her mother's conversion?
3. How does Scripture contrast how we see others with how God sees them? (see I Samuel 16:7)

Chapter Twenty-seven: Reunion

1. How did you feel reading about Madeline and Dave reconciling with their children?
2. Describe a time you were reconciled to someone. How did you see God's hand in that season?
3. What does Scripture say is the ministry of all those who have been reconciled to Christ? (see II Cor. 5:18-21)

ABOUT THE AUTHOR

Award-winning author, speaker, and Bible teacher Susan Carter was born in Halifax, Nova Scotia. She and her siblings moved to Kansas in 1973 and were adopted by Wayne and Bonnie Henley. Susan graduated from God's Bible School in Cincinnati, Ohio, with a BA in Music Education. In 2016, her dramatic life story was featured in a two-part series on the radio drama *Unshackled*.

Susan is passionate about Bible study and missions. When not engaged in ministry endeavors, you will find Susan playing with her grandchildren or working in her backyard garden. She lives in Goshen, Ohio, with her husband of thirty-four years, Gareth.

Susan is available to speak and especially enjoys sharing on the topics of salvation, forgiveness, healing from trauma, and issues around fostering and adoption. For younger audiences, her story of salvation is available in Sunday school/Vacation Bible School kit form. Visit Susan at www.SusanCarterAuthor.com to sign up for her ministry newsletter, learn more about her upcoming events, or contact her to speak to your group. Or you can contact her directly at 5Tickets2Kansas@gmail.com

Made in the USA
Columbia, SC
15 September 2024

41853135R00152